Schmitter

Rethinking America 1

★★★

An Intermediate Cultural Reader

D0080609

M. E. Sokolik
University of California, Berkeley

HH HEINLE & HEINLE PUBLISHERS
I(T)P™ *an International Thomson Publishing Company*

Boston – Albany – Bonn – Cincinnati – Detroit – London – Madrid –
Melbourne – Mexico City – New York – Pacific Grove – Paris –
San Francisco – Tokyo – Toronto – Washington

The publication of *Rethinking America 1, An Intermediate Cultural Reader* was directed by members of the Newbury House ESL/EFL Team at Heinle & Heinle Publishers:

Erik Gundersen: Senior Editor, ESL/ELT
Charlotte Sturdy: Market Development Director
Mike Burggren: Production Services Coordinator
Stanley J. Galek: Vice President and Publisher

Also participating in the publication of this program were:
Managing Developmental Editor: Amy Lawler
Developmental Editor: John Chapman
Assistant Editor: Jill Kinkade
Manufacturing Coordinator: Mary Beth Hennebury
Project Manager/Interior Designer: Linda Dana Willis
Cover Designer: Gina Petti
Cover Artist: Jasper Johns
Compositor: Modern Graphics, Inc.
For permission to use copyrighted material, grateful acknowledgment is made to the copyright holders on the Credits page, which are hereby made part of this copyright page.

ISBN: 0-8384-4750-3

Front cover illustration: JOHNS Jasper.
Map. (1961)
Oil on camvas, 6' 6" × 10' 3 1/8" (198.2 × 314.7 cm).
The Museum of Modern Art, New York. Gift of Mr. and Mrs. Robert C. Scull. Photograph © 1998 The Museum of Modern Art, New York.

ACKNOWLEDGMENTS

★★★

The fact that only my name appears on the cover seems a misrepresentation. Many, many people have helped in putting these volumes together. First and foremost, I would like to thank my Developmental Editor, John Chapman. His clarity of vision, insightful ideas, and masterful organization made this process much smoother than it otherwise would have been. Second, I would like to thank Erik Gundersen, Senior Editor, Heinle & Heinle for his unstinting support of the series and its expansion. I would also like to express my appreciation to Amy Lawler, Managing Developmental Editor, for doing such a great job in pulling all the pieces together and making sure everything was done right.

Other people at Heinle & Heinle have made valuable contributions as well. Joyce LaTulippe, Associate Developmental Editor, and Jonathan Boggs, Marketing Development Director, helped with the initial conception and development of the series. Jill Kinkade, Assistant Editor and Anne Sokolsky, Permissions Editor, dealt with the near-impossible task of getting rights to the authentic selections. And Becky Stovall, CNN Executive Producer in Atlanta, tracked down all the CNN video clips used in the series.

I also want to thank the reviewers and focus-group participants, whose insights and suggestions aided in the revision of the original text and in the conception of the two new volumes in the series:

Leslie Adams, Santa Ana College, CA

Alicia Aguirre, Cañada College, CA

Thom Allen, Chabot College, CA

Angelina Arellanes-Núñez, El Paso Community College, TX

Mardelle Azimi, California State University at Fullerton, CA

Victoria Badalamenti, LaGuardia Community College, NY

Gerald Lee Boyd, Northern Virginia Community College, VA

Pam Breyer, Braille Institute, CA

Mary Lou Byrne, Triton College, IL

Judi Camacho, Harper College, IL

Karen Carlson, Contra Costa College, CA

Jennifer Castello, Cañada College, CA

Anne Dorobis, Language Training Institute, NJ

Kathleen Flynn, Glendale Community College, CA

Ellen Clegg, ELS Language Center, CA

Patty Heiser, University of Washington Extension, WA

Jan Herwitz, ELS Language Center, San Francisco, CA

Gregory Keech, City College of San Francisco, CA

Julie Kim, University of Pennsylvania, PA

Tay Leslie, ELS Language Center, Los Angeles, CA

Kathleen Letellier, University of California Berkeley Extension, CA

Emily Lites, American Business English, CO

Robyn Mann, Harper College, IL

Roxanne Nuhaily, University of California, San Diego Extension, CA

Judith L. Paiva, Northern Virginia Community College, VA

Anita Razin, Santa Ana College, CA

Jan Rinaldi, Rio Hondo College, CA

Sandy Saldana, Triton College, IL

Irene Schoenberg, Hunter College, NY

Jane Selden, LaGuardia Community College, NY

Kathy Van Ormer, EDTP UAW-Ford National Programs Center, IL

Rose White, Lindsay Hopkins Technical Education Center, FL

James Wilson, Mount San Antonio College, CA

Finally, I want to thank every student who has ever said to me, "I don't understand." That statement alone has prompted me to try to put into writing answers to important questions. I hope I have succeeded.

—M. E. Sokolik

DEDICATION

★★

In memory of my aunt,
Chris Smith

CONTENTS

★★★

PREFACE

★★

Rethinking America is a multi-skill cultural series for students of English as a Second Language. Each book has ten broad topic areas. However, the subject matter in these areas varies from book to book. *Rethinking America* incorporates *authentic texts* as a source of reading. Authentic texts give the student an entry into understanding American culture by hearing authentic voices writing about their views and experiences. These readings also represent a variety of genres: newspaper articles and essays, poems, short stories, charts, graphs, and many others.

The readings and activities throughout *Rethinking America* foster cultural awareness, understanding, and interaction among students, and between students and their local setting, whether they are studying English in the U.S. or in another country. This series is intended to get students to examine not only American cultural values, but their own cultural values as well. Through these readings and activities, students engage in meaningful dialogues, and in the process, refine their English language skills.

Many of the changes and additions in this new edition stem from the thoughtful suggestions of students and teachers who have used *Rethinking America* over the years and from the suggestions of reviewers who carefully examined all three new manuscripts as we developed the series. It was extremely gratifying to be able to make use of these ideas as we expanded the original book into a three-book series.

This expansion involved several different types of changes. First of all, there are two new books at the intermediate and high-intermediate levels. Secondly, we have increased the scope of the reading comprehension sections, added specific reading strategies instruction in each chapter, and provided some exciting new ancillary components, including a video segment to accompany each chapter and an Almanac containing supplementary information at the back of each book. Thirdly, all follow-up activities now include exercises which are relevant to students who are using the book in a setting outside of the United States as well as within the U.S.

ORGANIZATION

Chapter Organization Each chapter is organized around a central theme and divided into two subthemes.

Each subtheme contains two readings that examine the topic from different points of view.

INTRODUCTORY MATERIALS

Before You Read Each reading is introduced by a photo, chart, or some other visual opener related to the reading topic. A brief preview of the reading follows, and students are encouraged to think about what they already know about the topic and to answer some questions about the preview.

Cultural Cues Information that may be culture-specific, such as references to television shows or historical figures, is explained before the reading.

About the Author Brief biographies of many of the authors are included. Photos of major figures in American culture are also provided.

THE READING

Each reading includes line numbers for easy reference by the student and teacher. In addition, some words are highlighted for quick reference.

Within each chapter, a video segment related to the topic and obtained from the CNN video archives is listed. Each video clip is accompanied by a set of suggested discussion questions.

EXPANSION MATERIALS

Check Your Comprehension Following each reading are five or more questions regarding the content of the reading.

Reading Strategy A specific reading strategy is highlighted in each follow-up reading activity. A brief statement about the strategy appears in a box in the margin along with a reference to the Reading Strategy Guide in the front of the book which contains a more complete explanation of the strategy.

Vocabulary In this section, students work with the vocabulary from the reading. The activities are varied and designed to keep the interest level high: some ask the students to think about the grammatical context of vocabulary, such as the use of prepositions in idiomatic phrases; some are matching and fill in the blank exercises; still others are games, such as word searches or crossword puzzles.

Think About It This section asks students to go beyond the factual content of a reading and relate their own knowledge and experience to the themes that are introduced. These questions sometimes ask students to apply their understanding to projects, such as participating in simulations, or looking at outside materials such as magazines and newspapers.

Synthesis   At the end of each chapter, a section of exercises and activities helps students integrate the ideas presented in the four readings of each chapter. These activities are designed to be relevant to students inside as well as outside the U.S.

Discussion and Debate   This section presents several questions that can be used for class discussion or debate. This activity encourages students to come up with their own questions, as well.

Writing Topics   The writing topics present different levels of writing tasks, from simple question-and-answer assignments or single-paragraph writing, to journal entries and short essays.

On Your Own   This section suggests projects that can be done outside of class. These activities include watching videos, conducting surveys, doing library or Internet research, as well as an array of other student-centered pursuits.

BONUS FEATURES

CNN Video Segments   Each volume of the *Rethinking America* series has an accompanying CNN video. The clips on this video are closely tied to one or more of the readings in the *Rethinking America* text. Questions are included in the text to foster discussion of the video. The video transcriptions are available and appear in the Instructor's Manual.

The Almanac   An almanac filled with stimulating and rich cultural information is found at the back of each book. It includes a list of major events in U.S. history, maps, temperature conversion tables, and other general information.

Instructor's Manual   An Instructor's Manual is available to help make best use of the features of *Rethinking America*. This Manual includes not only answer keys, but also tips for using the video segments, related Internet and other outside information, and guidelines for using the series in EFL settings. The transcriptions for the CNN video also appear in the Instructor's Manual.

Reference Guide to Reading Strategies

★★

Strategies

The following reading strategies are introduced and practiced in *Rethinking America 1:*

Drawing Conclusions Sometimes readings contain suggestions rather than direct statements. When this happens, you have to guess, or draw conclusions based on the information available to you.

Finding the Main Idea The main idea is the central, most important idea in the reading. Finding and understanding the main idea will help you understand the central purpose of the reading.

Increasing Speed By increasing your reading speed, you will actually understand more of what you are reading. When you increase your speed, you read words in groups, rather than individually. This helps you see the connections between the words and phrases in the reading.

Making Predictions When you make predictions, you use what you already know to make guesses about a reading before beginning the reading. Then, as you read, you check to see if your predictions were accurate. Predictions help you focus and prepare for the reading.

Reading Aloud Reading Aloud simply means speaking what you are reading, rather than reading silently. When you read aloud you hear the sound of words and phrases. Reading aloud can help you understand new words and information.

Scanning Scanning means reading quickly, without reading every word, in order to *find specific information* in a reading.

Skimming Skimming means reading quickly, without reading every word, in order to *get the main idea* of a reading. When you skim, look at titles, illustrations and anything else in a reading that will quickly give you information.

Summarizing   Summarizing means taking only the most important ideas and information from a reading and putting them in your own words. Try fitting your summaries on index cards.

___

Understanding by Categorizing   Categorizing means placing information into groups or categories. Putting ideas into two or more different categories can help you get a better understanding of the relationships between ideas in a reading.

___

Understanding from Context   Sometimes you can figure out the meaning of a new word or phrase by looking at the other words that come before and after it. These surrounding words can help to show the meaning of the new word or phase.

___

Understanding Examples   Examples are often used to support main ideas in a reading. Finding these examples will help give you a better understanding of the main points of a reading.

___

Understanding Facts and Opinions   A fact is something that is real and true. An opinion, on the other hand, is what a peson believes. An opinion has no proof. It is very important to make sure you understand when what you are reading is fact and when it is opinion.

___

Understanding Humor   Sometimes it can be difficult to understand the humor of another language and culture. However, by looking out for areas where the author exaggerates, or writes something which is clearly the opposite of what is true (sarcasm), you can often spot areas of humor in a reading.

___

Understanding Processes   A process is a sequence of related events. Understanding the process of events in a reading helps you see the order in which events happen. Look for words like "first," "second," "then," "next," and "finally" to help you understand a process.

___

Understanding Pronouns   A pronoun is a word that is used in place of a noun. For example, instead of referring to your sister by ame, you might use a pronoun such as "she," "her," or "hers." Recognizing when a pronoun is being used in place of a noun will help you to read more quickly and with better understanding.

★★

CHAPTER 1

The American Dream

"The American Dream" is a common phrase. However, its
definition is not simple. It is a complicated idea that mixes
hopes with history, ideas with ideals. What do you think
"The American Dream" means?

PART ONE

BEGINNINGS: Natives and Explorers

The American Dream is centuries old. Some believe that it came with the first European explorers. Others might say it was here even before that.

Before You Read

WHO FOUND IT?

 MERICA WAS DISCOVERED SO LONG AGO THAT NO ONE CAN REMEMBER THE DETAILS...

IT APPEARS TO HAVE HAPPENED ABOUT 15,000 YEARS AGO, WHEN A TRIBE OF SIBERIANS OR MONGOLIANS CROSSED A LAND BRIDGE THAT JOINED ASIA TO ALASKA AT THE TIME.

THE LAND BRIDGE SANK, AND THE VISITORS STAYED...

THIS SURE BEATS SIBERIA!

The first two readings are taken from the journals of Christopher Columbus and Amerigo Vespucci, an Italian explorer. Columbus is often called the "discoverer" of America. However, he only got as close as the Caribbean. Both men write about their impressions of the new world where they first landed.

Before you read this article, think about these questions:
- What do you know about Columbus?
- What do you know about the Caribbean islands?
- Have you heard of Amerigo Vespucci?

About the Authors

In Italian, he's *Cristoforo Colombo*, in Spanish, *Cristóbal Colón*. Christopher Columbus was born in 1451 and traveled to the New World for the first time in 1492. He planned to reach India by sailing west. He reached the Bahamas (October 12), then visited Cuba and Hispaniola (Haiti), where he left a small colony. He returned in 1493 and 1498, but was less successful. He died in Spain in 1506.

Amerigo Vespucci was an Italian explorer. He traveled to the New World after Columbus in 1499, and he explored the coast of Venezuela. He is said to have discovered the American mainland in 1497.

Paradise by Christopher Columbus

This is the most beautiful island I have ever seen. There are some large lakes, and around them is the most wonderful forest. The land around the river is covered with trees. They are beautiful and green and different from ours, each with flowers and fruit. The Indians' houses are the most beautiful
5   that I have ever seen. They are swept and very clean inside, and the furniture is nicely arranged. The evening air is sweet and **fragrant.**[1] The mountains are high and beautiful. This country is the best that language can describe.
  —1492

Gold is most excellent. Gold is a treasure! With gold, you can do whatever
10   you like in this world, even send **souls**[2] to heaven.
  —1495

[1]fragrant = sweet smelling
[2]souls = spirits

The New World by Amerigo Vespucci

First, I will describe the people. We found so many people here that we could not count them. They are gentle and friendly. They have large bodies, and their color is almost red. I think this is because they go naked, and they are red from the sun. They have long, black hair. They are attractive;
5   however, the men pierce their cheeks, lips, noses, and ears. They wear blue stones, beautiful **crystals**[1], and white bones in their **piercings**[2]. The women pierce only their ears.

They live together without a king or a government. They have no metal except gold, and we hear they have a lot of gold. However, we have not
10   seen any. The Indians do not value gold. They are also rich in **pearls**[3], and in birds, animals, and trees. If there is a **paradise**[4], I am sure it is not far from here.

Check Your Comprehension

1. What did Columbus like about the land he found?

2. What were the natives' houses like, according to Columbus?

3. How does Vespucci describe the natives?

4. What did Vespucci admire about the natives he met?

5. What does it mean that the men "pierce" their cheeks, lips, and noses?

6. How are these two readings similar?

 READING

Find out more about **scanning** by looking in the Reference Guide to Reading Strategies on pages xii–xiv.

Scanning

Scanning means to read something quickly for details. Scan the two explorers' reports. How are they similar? How are they different?

Scan the reading, then fill out the following table with information from the reading. Not all the ideas can be found in both readings.

[1]crystal = a type of clear stone
[2]piercings = holes
[3]pearls = round white jewels, produced by oysters
[4]paradise = perfect place

Idea	Columbus	Vespucci
Features of the land		
Physical features of the native people	XXXXXX	
What is said about gold		
Personality of the native people	XXXXXX	
Features of the native's homes		XXXXXX

VOCABULARY
Adjectives

Adjectives are words that describe nouns. For example, in the phrase "a red book," the word *red* is an adjective.

The following twelve adjectives are found in the readings. Review the reading if you don't know what they mean. Next to each word, write its antonym, or **opposite** meaning. More than one answer is possible. The first one is done for you.

1. *attractive* ____ ugly (or unattractive) _____
2. *clean* _____
3. *different* _____
4. *fragrant* _____
5. *friendly* _____
6. *gentle* _____
7. *high* _____
8. *large* _____
9. *long* _____
10. *naked* _____
11. *sweet* _____
12. *wonderful* _____

THINK ABOUT IT

1. Have you read about Columbus in history books? Is this reading different from what you have read?

2. Why do you think Americans celebrate Columbus Day, if Columbus didn't really discover America?

3. What is the history of your country? Was it discovered by an explorer? Or did it send explorers to discover other lands?

Before You Read

Some Wintu words:

soo coo = dog

luboles = wolf

suru surut = cricket

nawp = deer

 Watch the CNN Video about the Crazy Horse Monument. **Discuss these questions.**

1. Where is the monument?

2. Why is it important to Native Americans?

3. How long has it taken to create the monument?

In the next two readings, Native Americans talk about explorers coming to America. First, a Native American of the Wintu nation, talks about her view of the Europeans that came to explore her land. Then, Crazy Horse, a prominent member of the Sioux nation tells his story.

Before you read this story, think about these questions:

• What do you know about Native Americans?

• Have you seen any movies that show Native Americans?

• How do you think the Native Americans felt about the European explorers?

About The Authors The Holy Wintu Woman belonged to the nation of Wintu Natives in the state of California.

Crazy Horse was a mystic who was both admired and feared by many. He was the leader of the Oglala Sioux nation in the northern part of the United States. Crazy Horse led fights against European settlers. No photos exist of Crazy Horse, who thought that photographs trap the soul.

BY HOLY WINTU WOMAN THE SPIRIT OF THE LAND

The White people never cared for land or deer or bear. When we Indians kill meat, we eat it all up. When we dig roots we make little holes. When we build houses, we make little holes. When we burn grass for **grasshoppers**[1], we don't ruin things. We shake down **acorns**[2] and pine nuts. We don't
5 chop down the trees. We only use dead wood. But the White people **plow**[3] up the ground, pull down the trees, kill everything. The tree says, "Don't. I am sore. Don't hurt me." But they chop it down and cut it up. The spirit of the land hates them. They blast out trees and stir it up to its depths. They saw up the trees. That hurts them. The Indians never hurt anything, but the
10 White people destroy all. They blast rocks and scatter them on the ground. The rock says, "Don't. You are hurting me." But the White people pay no attention. When the Indians use rocks, they take little round ones for their cooking. . . . How can the spirit of the earth like the White man? . . . Everywhere the White man has touched it, it is sore.

[1]grasshopper = a jumping insect
[2]acorn = the nut of an oak tree
[3]plow = break up, turn

CIVILIZATION

BY CRAZY HORSE

We did not ask you white men to come here. The Great Spirit gave us this country as a home. You had yours. We did not **interfere**[1] with you. The Great Spirit gave us plenty of land to live on, and **buffalo**[2], deer, **antelope**[3] and other game. But you have come here; you are taking my land from me;

5 you are killing off our **game**[4], so it is hard for us to live. Now, you tell us to work for a living, but the Great Spirit did not make us to work, but to live by hunting. You white men can work if you want to. We do not interfere with you, and again you say, why do you not become civilized? We do not want your civilization! We would live as our fathers did, and their fathers

10 before them.

Check Your Comprehension

1. According to the Holy Wintu Woman, why do Native Americans hunt?

2. How do the Native Americans gather nuts?

3. Why does the Holy Wintu Woman think the "spirit of the land" hates White people?

4. Why does Crazy Horse think that White people should leave him alone?

5. How did "the white man" make it hard for Crazy Horse's people to live?

6. Why doesn't Crazy Horse want "civilization"?

7. Who is the Great Spirit?

[1]interfere with = bother, disrupt

[2]buffalo = large animals native to North America

[3]antelope = a type of deer

[4]game = wild animals used for food

READING

Find out more about **understanding examples** by looking in the Reference Guide to Reading Strategies on pages xii–xiv.

Understanding Examples

These writers make comparisons between the white people and the Native Americans. In doing so, they use **examples** to support their ideas. Fill out the following chart. Some of the examples require you to *draw conclusions* about what you have read. The first example is done for you.

Native Americans	White Explorers
Hunt to eat.	Kill for sport.

VOCABULARY
Crossword Puzzle

The answers to the clues are found in this chapter. Write the answers in the boxes.

Exploration

Across

2. The nut of an oak tree
3. What trees are made of
4. To set on fire
5. Fast, graceful animal
6. A grizzly or panda, for example
7. To cut with a tool which has a long blade
8. The part of a plant that takes in water
10. A jumping insect
13. To construct
14. To slice or chop
15. To move back and forth
16. Being without a body; ghost

Down

1. A pit made in the soil
2. A fast, deer-like animal
4. A cow-like animal
5. To ruin
9. To mix together
11. To sprinkle around
12. To tug
13. To knock down with explosives

THINK ABOUT IT

1. How do the two readings by Native Americans compare with those by Columbus and Vespucci?

2. What is "civilization," in your opinion? Why do you think the Native Americans rejected the idea of European civilization?

3. There are no photographs of Crazy Horse. He believed that photographs "stole pieces of his soul." Now there is a monument in his honor—a very large statue representing him. Do you think he would have approved of the statue? Why or why not?

PART TWO

The Pioneer Spirit: 🌵 Go West! 🌵

Part of the American Dream is the dream of moving. In the past, many people traveled from Europe and Asia to the United States in the hopes of finding a better life. For many of these immigrants, the American West held riches and new beginnings. The same is true today.

Before You Read

The Golden Gate Bridge in San Francisco

In this reading, an old man tells about moving to America from Japan. This was not an easy trip, as you will see. However, it was his dream.

Before you read, think about these questions:

- Have you ever moved to a new country or city? If so, what was the experience like?
- Have you ever been to San Francisco?

About the Author   Toshio Mori was born in Japan in 1910. He wrote the book *The Chauvinist and Other Stories*. He lives in Northern California.

by Toshio Mori

Yokohama, California

Long ago, children, I lived in a country called Japan. Your grandpa was already in California earning money for my boat ticket. The village people rarely went out of Japan and were shocked when they heard I was following your grandpa as soon as the money came.

5   "America!" they cried. "America is on the other side of the world! You will be in a strange country. You cannot read or write their language. What will you do?" I smiled, and in my dreams I saw the San Francisco your grandpa wrote about: San Francisco, the city with strange **enticing**[1] food; the city with gold coins; the city with many strange faces and music; the

10 city with great buildings and ships.

    One day his letter came with the money. "Come at once," he wrote. "Don't delay." The neighbors rushed excitedly to the house. "Don't go! Live among us," they cried. "There will be a war between America and Japan. You will be caught in mid-Pacific. You will never reach America." But I was

15 determined. They **painted**[2] the lonely lives of immigrants in a strange land. They cried on my shoulders and **embraced**[3] me. "I have bought my ticket and my things are packed. I am going," I said.

    The sea was rough, and I was sick almost all the way. There were others in the room just as ill. I couldn't touch the food. I began to have crazy

20 thoughts. Why was I going to America? Why had I been foolish enough to leave my village? For days I could not lift my head. Turn back? Did the ship turn back for me? No, child. A **steamer**[4] never turns back for an individual. Not for death or birth or storm. No more does life.

    When the boat finally passed the **Golden Gate**[5], I had my first **glimpse**[6]

25 of San Francisco. I was on **deck**[7] for hours, waiting for the golden city of dreams. I stood there with the other immigrants, chatting nervously and excitedly. First we saw only a thin shoreline. "America! America! We're in America!" someone cried.

[1]enticing = attractive, tempting

[2]painted = described

[3]embraced = hugged, held

[4]steamer = a boat that runs on steam power

[5]Golden Gate = the entrance to the San Francisco Bay from the Pacific Ocean

[6]glimpse = small view

[7]deck = top of the ship

Check Your Comprehension

1. Who is telling this story?

2. Why didn't the neighbors want the narrator to go to America?

3. What was the trip to America like?

4. What did the author know about San Francisco from his grandfather's letters?

5. What does the author mean in these sentences: "A steamer never turns back for an individual. Not for death or birth or storm. No more does life."

6. What were the narrator's "crazy thoughts"?

READING

Find out more about **drawing conclusions** by looking in the Reference Guide to Reading Strategies on pages xii–xiv.

Drawing Conclusions

There are some ideas in the reading that are not stated directly, but rather are suggested. From what the author tells the reader, what conclusions can you draw to answer these questions?

- Is the writer's grandfather happy with life in America?
- What do the village people think about America.
- What is the personality of the writer?

What parts of the story give you these ideas? Discuss your answers with your classmates.

VOCABULARY Using New Words

The words in **bold** are found in the text. Review your reading, then use a dictionary to look up any words you still don't understand. Show that you understand what the words mean by completing the following sentences.

1. When you are a student, you **rarely** _____ .

2. I was **shocked** when _____ .

3. The _____ was very **enticing**.

4. There was a **delay** when _____ .

5. She is very **determined** to _____ .

6. I **rushed** because _____ .

7. I felt **foolish** when I _____ .

8. When you see a **glimpse** of something, you see _____ .

9. We were **chatting** about _____ .

10. On the **shoreline** you may find many _____ .

THINK ABOUT IT

1. Have you ever wanted to do something that your friends were against your doing? Did you do it anyway? Why or why not?

2. Why do you think the author wanted to go to America? What might have influenced him?

3. Do you remember your thoughts the first time you saw America, or another place you have traveled to? What were those thoughts?

Before You Read

This reading is a poem about traveling by freight train. Reading poetry is a little different than reading an essay. You may need to read the poem more than once to understand it.

Before you read the poem, think about these questions:

- Have you read poetry in English before?
- Do you enjoy reading poetry?
- Have you traveled by train before? What was it like?

Cultural Cues

Great Northern   The name of a freight train company.

Fargo, North Dakota   A city in the northern part of the United States; this city was featured in the popular film *Fargo*.

About the Author

James Wright was born in 1927 and grew up in Martins Ferry, an industrial town on the Ohio River. He was raised in a working-class family during the poverty of the Great Depression. He developed a sympathy for criminals, minorities, and the uneducated that shows in his poetry. He died in 1980 in New York City.

❄ Outside Fargo, North Dakota ❄
by James Wright ❄

Along the **sprawled**[1] body of the **derailed**[2] **Great Northern** freight car,
I strike a match slowly and lift it slowly.
No wind.
Beyond town, three heavy white horses
5 Wade all the way to their shoulders
In a **silo**[3] shadow.

Suddenly the freight car **lurches**[4].
The door slams back, a man with a flashlight
Calls me good evening.
10 I nod as I write good evening, lonely
And sick for home.

Check Your Comprehension

1. What is the narrator doing?
2. What does the narrator see?
3. Who calls "good evening" to him?
4. How does the narrator feel?

[1]sprawled = stretched or spread on the ground
[2]derailed = a train derails when it goes off its tracks
[3]silo = a farm building used for storing grain
[4]lurches = moves forward suddenly

**READING**

Find out more about **reading aloud** by looking in the Reference Guide to Reading Strategies on pages xii–xiv.

Reading Aloud

In order to understand a poem, it helps to **read it out loud.** Practice reading the poem aloud. Pay attention to the punctuation in order to understand where sentences begin and end.

VOCABULARY
Using New Verbs

These verbs are found in the poem and might be new to you. Review the poem to be sure you understand these verbs. Then, draw a line from the verb to the word that is similar in meaning.

1. *derail*   stretch

2. *lurch*   go off track

3. *slam*   light

4. *sprawl*   walk in water

5. *strike*   jerk forward

6. *wade*   close
                  violently

THINK ABOUT IT

1. What feeling do you get from the poem? Why?

2. Who do you think the narrator is? Why do you think this?

3. Have you ever traveled alone? What was it like?

SYNTHESIS

Discussion and Debate

1. Many people think Columbus is a hero because he "discovered" America. Others think he does not deserve to be called a hero because he didn't really land in what is now called America, and he took land from the Indians. What do you think?

2. Some people think there are too many immigrants in the United States. What do you think? Should America continue to accept immigrants?

3. Why is movement and migration part of the American Dream, in your opinion?

4. Ask your classmates another question that you have about the ideas in this chapter.

Writing Topics   1.   Write a letter to a friend or family member about what you have learned about Native Americans.

2.   In your journal, write about your understanding of the American Dream. Support your ideas with examples.

3.   Do you have a dream? What is it? Write a short essay explaining it.

On Your Own   1.   Ask five people the following questions. Write their answers in the table. Compare your answers to your classmates'.

Question	Person 1 Name:	Person 2 Name:	Person 3 Name:	Person 4 Name:	Person 5 Name:
1. Should Americans celebrate Columbus Day? Why or why not?					
2. Do you think Native Americans have been treated fairly in the United States?					
3. Do you think America has too many immigrants?					
4. What is the American Dream?					

2.   Go to the library or use the Internet to find out more about Columbus, Native Americans, or immigration. Report to your class on what you find.

3.   Many films have been made about Columbus, Native Americans, and immigrating to the United States. Watch one of these films and report on it to your class.

1492: Conquest of Paradise (1992)

Dances with Wolves (1990)

Little Big Man (1970)

Moscow on the Hudson (1984)

Green Card (1990)

★★

A L M A N A C   For additional cultural information, refer to the Almanac on pages 207–222. The Almanac contains lists of useful facts, maps, and other information to enhance your learning.

★★

CHAPTER 2

Money

Money plays an important role in everyone's life. However, each culture has its own attitudes and feelings about money. This chapter looks at money in America—at home and at work.

PART ONE

Housing: Home Sweet Home

In the United States, the largest purchase most people make is their home. The majority of American families own their own homes. These homes are symbols of independence and self-sufficiency.

Before You Read

Appliances and Features of U.S. Households

Feature	Percentage of Households
Color television set	98
Microwave oven	84
Clothes washer	77
Clothes dryer	72
Air conditioning	68
Dishwasher	45
Swimming pool	5

Source: *U.S. Dept. of Energy Annual Energy Review*

The following reading is about how home designs are changing. Before you read this think about the following questions:

• What features are most important to you in a home?

• Is owning a home important to you?

• Look at the table: are you surprised that more people have televisions than clothes washers? Does anything else in the table surprise you?

Cultural Cues

Baby boomers People born after World War II up until 1964; it is called a "boom" because there was a large increase in the number of births in these years. Baby boomers still represent a very large part of the American population. Therefore, they greatly influence the politics and economy of the country.

About the Author   Patricia Edmonds is a *USA Weekend* associate editor.

Your Dream House
by Patricia Edmonds

A new generation is changing the plan for the great American dream home. Their ideas reflect today's values.

The big, open kitchen in the center of the
5 house says: *We love our time with family*. The stress-free **master bedroom**[1] with a bathtub and private parlor says: *We still need time away to relax*. A high-tech home office states: *We keep one eye on work*. But a welcoming
10 front **porch**[2] insists: *We want to feel connected, to be neighbors*.

Baby boomers (the 78 million Americans born 1946-64) make the **trends**[3] in home design. When baby boomers build their dream
15 homes, they demand "much more than basic shelter," says designer Carole Eichen. "We're no longer selling homes to people; we're selling lifestyles." Mark and Lorene Heinze are buying.

Their 2,300-square-foot new house near De-
20 troit has the latest features: a big bathtub, extra storage, and high ceilings. "When I walk into my house," Lorene says, "I think, 'I just love it.'"

757,000 U.S. families bought new homes in
25 1996, the best year for sales of new homes since 1978. Buying a dream home is a fantasy with a variable price tag. A house like the Heinzes' costs about $250,000 in the Detroit area, $120,000 in Houston, $205,000 in Denver,
30 $323,000 in Boston and $338,000 in northern California.

Baby-boomers may see their dream home differently from homebuyers born before or after them. However, some design features ap-
35 peal to all generations. These new designs appear first in luxury houses in trend-setting California. Once they become popular, builders modify them for lower price ranges and copy them nationwide.

40 So Mark Heinze is working in his home near Detroit, making his unfinished basement into a playroom, a woodworking shop, and a home office. This house fulfills his dream: "I wanted to feel, when I came home from work, that I'm
45 on vacation," he says. "This house is everything I wanted and more."

Source: *USA Today*

---

[1]master bedroom = the largest bedroom in the house, usually occupied by the parents in a family.

[2]porch = an open area in front of a house

[3]trends = tendencies, directions, fashions

Check Your Comprehension

1. What are "baby boomers"?

2. According to the reading, what does a "big, open kitchen" mean?

3. What does a big "stress-free master bedroom" symbolize?

4. What is a "high-tech" home?

5. Why do some people want a front porch?

6. How are baby boomers' housing desires different from other generations'?

7. What does the sentence, "Buying a dream home is a fantasy with a variable price tag" mean?

8. In what state are fashions for houses started?

9. Why was 1996 special for homebuyers?

READING

Find out more about **scanning** by looking in the Reference Guide to Reading Strategies on pages xii–xiv.

Scanning

Scanning means looking over a reading for specific information. Scan the article and complete this table of information.

1. The number of baby-boomers: _____

2. Three popular features in new homes: _____
_____
_____
_____

3. The number of families who bought new homes in 1996: _____

4. The "baby boom" years: _____

VOCABULARY
Housing Vocabulary

This article contains several vocabulary items that are special "housing vocabulary". Answer the following questions about these vocabulary items.

1. Where in a house do you find a **porch**?_____
_____

2. What might you do in a **parlor**? _____
_____

3. How is a **master bedroom** different from other kinds of bedrooms?
_____

4. Name the types of **storage** areas you might find in a house. _____
_____

5. Where do you find **ceilings** in a house? _____
_____

6. Who would use a **playroom**? _____
_____

7. What things would you find in a **home office**? _____

_____

8. What would you do in a **woodworking shop**? _____

_____

9. Where in a house is the **basement**? _____

_____

THINK ABOUT IT

1. How do houses in the United States compare houses in other countries?

2. What is your dream home like? What features would you like to have in your house? If you can, draw a sketch of it and share it with your classmates.

3. Look through magazines such as *Better Homes and Gardens, Metropolitan Home,* or *Architectural Digest.* What features do you see? What do you think of the homes that are pictured?

Before You Read

U.S. Households

Total Number of Households	91,947,410
Total Number of Families	64,517,947
Nonfamily Households	27,429,463
People Living Alone	22,580,420
People in Group Households	3,363,726
Average Number of People per Household	2.63

Source: Bureau of the Census

 Watch the CNN video about co-housing.
Discuss these questions.

1. According to the video, what is co-housing?

2. What kinds of people live in co-housing?

3. What activities do the co-housing residents do together?

The following reading is about co-housing, a new trend in American housing.

Before you read, think about the following questions:

• Do you know what "communal" means?

• Do you prefer living alone, or with other people?

• Look at the last line of the table. Do you think households in your country are larger or smaller than this, on average?

• What do you think "nonfamily household" means in the table?

WWW ED.GOV.
MONEY PIT

Cultural Cues   *hippie* A person, usually identified with the 1960s, who rejects traditional values and lifestyles.

What is Co-Housing ?

In many countries, it is not unusual for families of different backgrounds to live together in shared space. However, in the United States, this idea may still be considered odd.

5 But this type of housing, called co-housing, is gaining popularity in the United States, too. Co-housing **complexes**[1] are popping up in cities across the country. For many people, this way of life is a relief to the busy modern life-
10 style. About 25 co-housing communities have been built in recent years, and 150 more are planned.

In co-housing complexes, everyone helps take care of children and elderly residents. It's
15 also a place where residents shop, cook, and eat together. Residents of co-housing complexes like its sense of shared community.

Children have other kids to play with, which many families like. Other residents like the feel-
20 ing of living in a "village." Residents also say that they can live in co-housing for less money than they would pay for nearby apartments.

Some people may think that co-housing might be like a 1960s **"hippie" commune**[2].
25 But after they learn about it, they change their minds. This is because privacy is still important to residents. They have individual houses, not one big house, as old-style communes did. Although they share the responsibilities of the
30 community, each family still lives its own life.

Will this trend catch on? It probably will never become the most popular form of housing in the United States, but for many, it's the answer to many of the problems of a busy mod-
35 ern life.

[1]complexes = groups

[2]commune = housing that is shared by more than one family. The work and childcare responsiblities are usually shared in a commune.

Check Your Comprehension

1. What is co-housing?

2. How are co-housing complexes and communes different?

3. How many co-housing communities are there in the United States?

4. How popular is co-housing in the United States?

5. Why do residents of co-housing like it?

6. What are the advantages of co-housing, according to the article?

READING

Find out more about **understanding by categorizing** by looking in the Reference Guide to Reading Strategies on pages xii–xiv.

Understanding by Categorizing

This reading gives you basic information about co-housing. **Categorize** that information by putting it into the following chart. You may add boxes or arrows if you think they are needed.

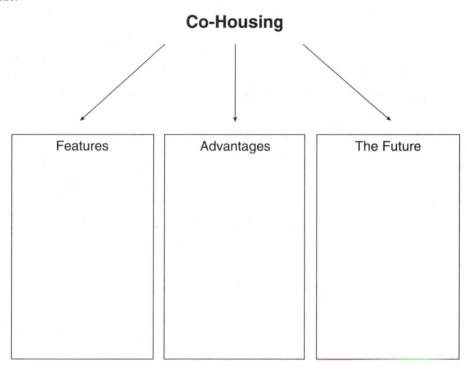

Co-Housing

Features	Advantages	The Future

VOCABULARY
New Words

Review the reading, looking for the words in this list. If you don't know their meanings, look them up in your dictionary, or discuss them with a classmate. Then, fill in the blanks with the correct words from the following list.

backgrounds	*odd*	*relief*
commune	*popping*	*shared*
gaining	*privacy*	*trend*
nearby	*recent*	*village*

1. _____ is still important to co-housing residents.

2. About 25 co-housing communities have been built in

   _____ years.

3. Co-housing communities are _____ up across the country.

4. Co-housing is _____ popularity in the United States.

5. For many people, co-housing is a _____ to the busy modern lifestyle.

6. In some countries, families with different _____ live together in shared space.

7. In the United States, co-housing may still be considered

   _____ .

8. Residents can live in co-housing for less than

   _____ apartments.

9. Residents of co-housing like its sense of _____ community.

10. Some co-housing residents like the feeling of living in a

    _____ .

11. Some people believe that co-housing is like a hippie

    _____ .

12. Will the co-housing _____ catch on?

THINK ABOUT IT

1. What kind of housing do you prefer—a house, or an apartment? Living with other people or alone? Why?

2. Do you think your family would enjoy co-housing? Why or why not?

3. The table at the beginning of the chapter states that the average household size is 2.63 in the United States. Do you think this is small or large? How does it compare to households in your home country?

PART TWO

WORK: It's My Job

In order to earn money, people work. However, work is important for more than just money. It also offers the opportunity for people to show their skill, while meeting and making friends. However, it is also a source of unhappiness for many people.

Before You Read

A company seminar

A company outing

In the following reading, the author shares e-mail messages he received from workers. These workers are describing real events that happened at work.

Before you read these messages, look at the photographs on the previous page. Then, answer these questions:

- Why do you think a company would have a picnic?
- What kinds of ideas might be shared in a seminar?
- If you have a job, do you enjoy your work?
- Why do you think many people dislike their jobs?

Cultural Cues

VP Vice President.

aol.com The Internet address of America On-line, the most popular e-mail and Internet provider in the United States.

CEO Chief Executive Officer, another name for the head of a company.

About the Author

Scott Adams worked in an office for many years before becoming a cartoonist and humor writer. His books and comic strips, featuring "Dilbert," show the silly and difficult side of office life. He lives in Northern California.

E-MAIL MESSAGES
BY SCOTT ADAMS

From: (name withheld)

To: scottadams@aol.com

Scott,

Here's a funny disaster **scenario**[1], a true situation that happened at a company I worked at. The president of the company decided we needed **an off-site**[2]. He decided that an ideal off-site was a bike ride. He chose a thirty-mile route and handed out hand-drawn maps.

Half the company didn't have bikes and rented them.

---

[1] scenario = story, outline
[2] an off-site = an activity away from the workplace, usually for fun and to build morale

Nobody was **in shape**[3]. The route turned out to be fairly hilly (and thirty miles is a long ride even in flat **terrain**[4] for someone who doesn't ride regularly). The map was wrong and nobody had real maps. Several people got lost and never made it to lunch. One person ended up in the hospital (he **collapsed**[5] due to low **blood sugar**[6] while biking up a hill). The planned discussions and activities for the day never happened. And the president didn't understand until days later how much of a disaster the day had been. After all, he'd enjoyed his ride.

From: (name withheld)

To: scottadams@aol.com

Scott,

True story:
When we were **down in the dumps**[7] one year, our newish CEO decided that we needed a **motivational**[8] meeting, complete with professional **corporate**[9] motivation video. The video featured the "try again until success" attitude of **balloonist**[10] Maxie Anderson and was coordinated with a personal letter from the famed balloonist.
(Maxie had been killed three years earlier in a ballooning accident.)

Check Your Comprehension

1. What's an "off-site"?

2. What kind of off-site was planned in the first message?

3. What was wrong with the maps at the off-site?

4. Why did some people have difficulty bicycling?

---

[3]in shape = physically fit

[4]terrain = ground

[5]collapsed = fainted, fell

[6]blood sugar = the amount of sugar in your blood, which gives you energy

[7]down in the dumps = sad

[8]motivational meeting = a meeting or seminar to help people get more excited and enthusiastic about their work

[9]corporate = relating to the company or corporation

[10]balloonist = someone who flies large hot-air balloons

5. Why was the boss happy with the off-site?

6. Why did the workers in the second message need a "motivational meeting"?

7. Who was Maxie Anderson?

8. In the second message, why wasn't the motivational meeting a success?

 READING

Find out more about **drawing conclusions** by looking in the Reference Guide to Reading Strategies on pages xii–xiv.

Drawing Conclusions

Certain ideas in the reading are not explained, but you can **draw conclusions** about them. What conclusions can you make about the following questions?

1. What does "name withheld" mean at the top of the e-mail messages? Why do you think the author withheld the name?

   _____

   _____

2. Why would a boss think an off-site was a good idea?

   _____

   _____

3. What happens at an off-site?

   _____

   _____

4. What do American bosses do to motivate their workers?

   _____

   _____

VOCABULARY
Understanding New Vocabulary

Review the reading. Look at the following phrases in **bold.** Do you know what they mean? Discuss them with a classmate, or look them up in a dictionary. Then, choose the sentence that means the same as the original.

1. Does it ever **cross your mind** to quit your job?

   a. Do you ever get angry about your job?

   b. Do you ever consider quitting your job?

   c. Have you ever quit your job?

2. My friend is feeling **down in the dumps.**

   a. My friend is feeling angry.

   b. My friend is feeling sick.

   c. My friend is feeling sad.

3. I need to get **in shape.**

   a. I need to clean my room.

   b. I need to wear nicer clothes.

   c. I need to improve my health.

4. It will be difficult to **make it** to school in this weather.

   a. It will be difficult to get to school because of the bad weather.

   b. It will be difficult in school today because of the weather.

   c. It will be difficult to stay in school because of the weather.

5. We had a big dinner, **complete with** dessert and coffee.

   a. We finished dinner by having dessert and coffee.

   b. We had a large meal which included dessert and coffee.

   c. No dinner is complete without dessert and coffee.

6. One person **ended up** in the hospital.

   a. Someone visited the hospital.

   b. Someone died in the hospital.

   c. Someone had to go to the hospital.

THINK ABOUT IT

1. If you have had any jobs, what were your bosses like?

2. Have you ever quit a job? Why?

3. Why do you think people often complain about work?

4. Should employers plan employee picnics and parties? Why?

5. What kinds of activities do you think might motivate employees?

Before You Read

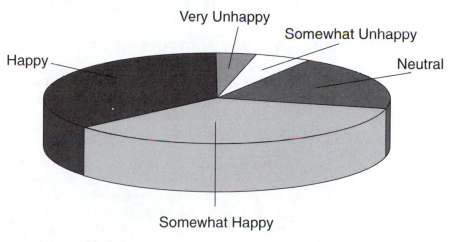

Worker Satisfaction

Very Unhappy

Somewhat Unhappy

Happy

Neutral

Somewhat Happy

This pie chart shows that most American workers are happy with their jobs. In fact, 71 percent are either happy or somewhat happy with their jobs. The following reading, however, talks about what happens when workers aren't happy.

Before you read, think about these questions:

- What does "sabotage" mean?
- What would you do if you were treated badly at work?

a bicycle messenger

SABOTAGE IN THE WORKPLACE

by Martin Sprouse

Kitchen Manager—Wez

I had been working at a café called Pacific Desserts for two years. One day the kitchen manager quit. I had worked there the longest. I was given the kitchen manager's work, but not the **title**[1] or the pay.

5　High school kids waited tables at night there. They often visited in the morning before the place was open. They came for free coffee. I had been making myself breakfast before the manager got there and I decided to expand. For the last three months of school, I made omelettes and fried potatoes using the restaurant's eggs, cheese, milk, vegetables, potatoes, and

10　spices. We started a morning coffee club, and charged $1 per plate. Soon the high school students started to bring their friends. One of them even made a **plaque**[2] in his pottery class that read "Wez's Underground Café." I usually made about $8 extra per day. This was the same as a **raise**[3]. I was also spending an hour of the company's time for my own profit.

15　*Bicycle Messenger—Kenny*

Being a bike messenger in Seattle is hard, but our job was easy. We had to **work our butts off**[4], but at least we got paid by the hour.

The company always let us wear shorts, but we had to wear the company T-shirts. We cut off the sleeves to stay cool. Then, the company wanted to

20　**clean up its image**[5] because we delivered to big businesses. They made us wear long pants and shirts made of heavy material. This was crazy! Try riding your bicycle fast for ten miles up hills, really big hills, with heavy packages while you're wearing long pants!

All of the messengers agreed we could not continue like that. We decided

25　that we wouldn't wash our clothes at all. We wore the same clothes every day. You can imagine what it was like when we were in an elevator. Our clothes were stinking and our bodies were stinking. Within a month, the company received many complaints. They let us wear shorts again.

---

[1]title = job title, which shows the status of the worker

[2]plaque = sign

[3]raise = increase in salary

[4]work our butts off = work extremely hard

[5]clean up its image = present itself better than before

Check Your Comprehension

1. How was Wez being treated unfairly at his job?

2. Why was Kenny unhappy at his job?

3. Why is it difficult to be a bicycle messenger in Seattle?

4. Why did Kenny's company change its rules on clothing?

5. What was Wez's sabotage?

6. What was Kenny's sabotage?

7. Why did the messenger company want to "clean up its image"?

8. How did the messenger company respond to the employee's protest?

 **READING**

Find out more about **understanding pronouns** by looking in the Reference Guide to Reading Strategies on pages xii–xiv.

Understanding Pronouns

In English, one doesn't typically repeat the same noun when it is referred to soon after its first mention. For example: *Manuel is my friend. He is the same age as me.* The word *he* is a pronoun that refers to Manuel. It is not necessary to repeat the name "Manuel."

Using **pronouns** makes writing and reading more *economical*. Pronouns are usually shorter than nouns, and are a shorthand way of referring to things.

Here are some passages from the reading. Underline all the personal pronouns *(I/me, he/him, she/her, they/them, we/us, it)* and **possessive** pronouns *(my, his, hers, their, our, its)*. Then, circle and draw a line from the noun they refer to. The first one is done as an example.

1. High school (kids) waited tables at night there. They often visited in the morning before the place was open. They came for free coffee.

2. Soon the high school students started to bring their friends. One of them even made a plaque in his pottery class that read "Wez's Underground Café."

3. The company always let us wear shorts, but we had to wear the company T-shirts. We cut off the sleeves to stay cool. They made us wear long pants and shirts made of heavy material.

4. All of the messengers agreed we could not continue like that. We decided that we wouldn't wash our clothes at all. We wore the same clothes every day.

5. Within a month, the company received many complaints. They let us

wear shorts again.

**VOCABULARY
Using a Dictionary**

Find these ten words in an English-English dictionary. Write the definition for each in your own words. Include an example sentence. Write with a pencil to begin, as you may want to change your answers.

1. *manager*

Definition: _____

Example sentence: _____

_____

2. *omelette*

Definition: _____

Example sentence: _____

_____

3. *plaque*

Definition: _____

Example sentence: _____

_____

4. *pottery*

Definition: _____

Example sentence: _____

_____

5. *underground*

Definition: _____

Example sentence: _____

_____

6. *raise* (noun)

Definition: _____

Example sentence: _____

_____

7. *profit*

Definition: _____

Example sentence: _____

_____

8. *sleeve*

Definition: _____

Example sentence: _____

_____

9. *elevator*

Definition: _____

Example sentence: _____

_____

10. *complaint*

Definition: _____

Example sentence: _____

_____

Compare your answers with a partner's. How are your answers different? Rewrite your answers if you want.

THINK ABOUT IT

1. Do you agree with the actions the workers took? Why or why not?

2. What should workers do when they feel their bosses are not being fair?

3. What kind of job would you hate to have? What kind would you love to have?

S Y N T H E S I S

Discussion and Debate

1. How hard would you work for the house of your dreams? Would you work long hours? Would you work two jobs? Explain your answer to your classmates.

2. Many people say that Americans care too much about money. Do you agree? How do Americans' attitudes toward money compare to attitudes in your country?

3. Is a home the same as a house? If not, explain the difference.

4. Think of another question to ask your classmates about the ideas in this chapter.

Writing Topics

1. In your journal, write about your dream job. What would you like to do? How much money would you like to make?

2. Write a letter to a friend or family member and describe your housing situation. Explain what kind of house or apartment you live in, what is good and bad about it, and any other details you would like to include.

3. Choose one of the following topics, and write an essay defending your point of view. Be sure to use examples to show your point.

   a. Working for a big company is better than working for a small one.

   b. Working for a small company is better than working for a big one.

   c. Living in an apartment is better than living in a house.

   d. Living in a house is better than living in an apartment.

On Your Own 1. Conduct your own "job satisfaction" survey. Ask ten workers this question: How happy are you with your job?

| 1–very unhappy | 3–not happy or unhappy | 5–very happy |
| 2–unhappy | 4–happy | |

Mark your answers in this chart:

Person	1 Very Unhappy	2 Unhappy	3 Not Unhappy or Happy	4 Happy	5 Very Happy
1.					
2.					
3.					
4.					
5.					
6.					
7.					
8.					
9.					
10.					

Count up your answers and compare them with your classmates'. How do your results compare to the results on page 33 of this chapter?

2. Interview someone about his or her job. Prepare ten questions that you will ask. During the interview, be sure to take notes, or ask permission to tape record the interview. Write it up and report to the class.

3. Watch two television shows that feature people at home and working. What shows did you watch? Complete the following descriptions. Report to your class.

Television Show 1

Program title: _____

Main character: _____

Type of job: _____

Description of house or apartment: _____

The plot: _____

Television Show 2

Program title: _____

Main character: _____

Type of job: _____

Description of house or apartment: _____

The plot: _____

How do the two shows compare? _____

_____

_____

_____

_____

★★

A L M A N A C   For additional cultural information, refer to the Almanac on pages 207–222. The Almanac contains lists of useful facts, maps, and other information to enhance your learning.

★★★

CHAPTER 3

Traditions

Every culture has its own traditions. In fact, traditions are what make a culture unique. This chapter looks at two types of American traditions related to weddings and food.

PART ONE

WEDDINGS: Here Comes the Bride!

Weddings are happy events in every culture. This section contains a reading about the way a traditional American bride dresses, as well as a poem about the events that took place after one man's wedding.

Before You Read

Groom and bride in traditional wedding clothes

The following reading discusses the symbolic meaning of the bride's clothing on her wedding day.

Before you read this article, think about the following questions:

- What are wedding traditions like in your country?
- What does the bride wear?

- What does the groom wear?
- Have you ever been to a wedding from a different culture? What was it like?

Something Old, Something New

Although weddings vary greatly in the United States, in most American weddings, the bride follows certain traditions of dress. Here's what she'll wear or carry.

Something Old

5   There is an old saying that tells women what they should wear or carry when they marry:

"Something old, something new, something borrowed, something blue"

This good luck saying dates back to Victorian times in the 1800s, and many American brides try to dress according to this saying.

10   "Something old" symbolizes the connection with the bride's family and the past. Many brides wear a piece of family jewelry or a mother's or grandmother's wedding dress.

"Something new" symbolizes good luck and success in the bride's new life. The wedding dress is often the new item. However, the bride may wear

15   new jewelry or new shoes.

"Something borrowed" reminds the bride that friends and family will help her when she needs it. The borrowed object might be something such as a lace handkerchief, or a best friend's bridal **veil**[1].

"Something blue" is the symbol of faithfulness and loyalty. Often the

20   blue item is the **garter**[2] worn on the bride's leg. It might also be a ribbon or a piece of jewelry.

The Bouquet

The bride carries flowers as a symbol of happiness. In the past, both the bride and groom wore flowers. At the end of the wedding **reception**[3],

25   the bride tosses her bouquet to all the single women who attend the party. The single woman who catches the bouquet is believed to be the next to marry.

[1]veil = a piece of transparent cloth worn on the head, sometimes over the bride's face.
[2]garter = an elastic band worn around the leg to hold up socks or stockings.
[3]reception = party

The Garter

30 Throwing the garter began in France when pieces of the bride's clothing were considered lucky. The bride would throw the garter to the guests at the wedding and whoever caught it could expect good luck. In the United States, the groom traditionally removes the garter from the bride and throws it to the unmarried men. The man who catches it is thought to be the next to marry. At some weddings, the man who catches the garter will place it 35 on the leg of the woman who caught the bouquet, or they may start the next dance. It is also common for the recipients of the bouquet and garter to have their photo taken with the bride and groom.

Whatever the bride wears, it is also traditional that she be the best-dressed and most important woman at the wedding party. So, it is considered 40 very impolite for other women at the wedding to dress more beautifully than the bride.

Check Your Comprehension

1. What old saying tells how brides should dress at their weddings?

2. What does "something old" symbolize? What is a typical "old" item worn by a bride?

3. What does "something new" symbolize? What is a typical "new" item worn by a bride?

4. What does "something borrowed" symbolize? What is a typical "borrowed" item worn by a bride?

5. What does "something blue" symbolize? What is a typical "blue" item worn by a bride?

6. What is a garter?

7. What is done with the garter at a wedding?

8. What do flowers symbolize at a wedding?

9. What is done with the wedding bouquet?

10. What is believed to happen to the people who catch the garter and bouquet?

11. How should a woman dress at her friend's wedding?

 **READING**

Find out more about **summarizing** by looking in the Reference Guide to Reading Strategies on pages xii–xiv.

Summarizing

Summarizing means rewriting a story or an essay so that just the most important parts are included. Although this reading is already short, it is possible to remove some of the details to make it shorter, while keeping the most important details.

Look at the first two paragraphs, repeated here:

There is an old saying that tells women what they should wear or carry when they marry:

"Something old, something new, something borrowed, something blue"

This good-luck saying dates back to Victorian times in the 1800s, and many American brides try to dress according to this saying.

What information is less important? What information is very important? In the following paragraphs the important information is in **bold.** The less important information is crossed out.

~~There is~~ **an old saying** ~~that~~ **tells women what they should wear** ~~or carry~~ **when they marry:**

"Something old, something new, something borrowed, something blue"

~~This good-luck saying dates back to~~ **Victorian** ~~times in the 1800s, and many~~ **American brides try to dress according to this saying.**

To write a summary, you would then write the important information from above in your own words:

An old, Victorian saying tells American brides how to dress. That saying is, "Something old, something new, something borrowed, something blue."

Compare the original and the summary. Answer these questions:

1. How was it rewritten?

2. What information was kept, and what was left out?

3. You may not agree with the way the summary was done. Would you have included that it is a "good-luck" saying? Why or why not?

Summarize the rest of the story. Use the following space (and no more!).

_____

_____

_____

_____

Then, compare your summary to a classmate's. Answer these questions:

5. What information did you include that your classmate did not?

6. What did you leave out?

7. Now that you have read your classmate's summary, do you want to change yours?

VOCABULARY
A Wedding Word Search

Write a brief explanation of the words listed below. Then, look for these words, which are associated with weddings, in the grid and circle them (be sure to check them off the list when you find them). You will find the words going forward, backwards, and diagonally. The first one is done for you.

1. √ *bride* _____

2. *groom* _____

3. *bouquet* _____

4. *garter* _____

5. *gown* _____

6. *reception* _____

7. *wedding*

8. *blue* _____

9. *borrowed* _____

10. *veil* _____

R	W	N	D	P	S	P	Q	T	Z
J	E	U	L	B	I	H	D	R	E
M	D	C	E	M	F	G	E	E	T
A	D	C	E	D	O	M	W	T	G
B	I	D	M	P	J	O	O	R	B
V	N	T	Z	A	T	A	R	A	J
E	G	E	R	V	R	I	R	G	I
Z	W	T	E	U	Q	U	O	B	P
Q	Y	I	E	D	I	R	B	N	O
S	L	R	B	Q	T	G	O	W	N

THINK ABOUT IT

1. How does a bride dress in a traditional wedding in your culture? How is it different from the traditional American dress?

2. Are there any sayings associated with weddings in your language? What are they? What do they mean?

3. White is a symbol of purity at weddings. What colors are symbolic in weddings in your culture? What do they mean?

4. Have you attended a wedding? What was it like? Did you enjoy it?

Before You Read

A Jewish wedding

Cultural Cues

crush my wedding glass beneath my shoe Part of a Jewish wedding ceremony; this action is usually done by the man and signals the end of the formal ceremony. After the crushing of the glass, the people attending the wedding usually shout *"L'chaim!"* which means "to life!"

Jehoshaphat The king of Judah (c.873-849 B.C.), who was the first king of Judah to make a treaty with the kingdom of Israel; his name is often used as an exclamation, "Jumping Jehoshaphat."

About the Author James Reiss' poems have appeared in many magazines, such as *The Atlantic Monthly* and *The New Yorker*. He is the author of three books of poems, *The Breathers, Express,* and *The Parable of Fire.* He is Professor of English at Miami University in Oxford, Ohio.

◆ ◆ ◆ ◆ CYCLE ◆ ◆ ◆ ◆

BY JAMES REISS

What why when where who
I crush my wedding glass beneath my shoe

In with from to at
I kiss my bride & cry **Jehoshaphat**

5   Five four three two one
I father daughters & **entomb**[1] a son

Minsk Flint Perth Seoul Rome
I travel far to find myself at home

Large **squat**[2] thin fat small
10   I greet a stranger in a shopping mall

Taste touch smell hear see
I lose my wife my gentle Melanie

I take my life & shake it by the hair
Who what why when where

[1]entomb = bury after death, put into a tomb
[2]squat = short, usually a little fat

Check Your Comprehension

1. Who is the **narrator** of this poem?

2. This poem is written in **couplets,** or verses of two lines each. What is the purpose of the first line in each couplet?

3. What is the purpose of the second line in each couplet?

4. What is the meaning of "I greet a stranger in a shopping mall"? Why has the poet included this detail, in your opinion?

5. Who was Melanie?

6. What does the poet mean by "I take my life & shake it by the hair"?

7. What is the **mood** of this poem (happy, sad, etc.)?

8. How is the last couplet different from the earlier ones in the poem? Why do you think the author wrote it differently?

9. Why is this poem called "Cycle"?

READING

Find out more about **reading aloud** by looking in the Reference Guide to Reading Strategies on pages xii–xiv.

Reading Aloud

Reading aloud helps you to better understand poetry. Practice reading the poem aloud. Listen carefully to the rhythm and the sounds of the words.

**VOCABULARY
Prepositions**

The author of this poem uses many **prepositions** to show the relationship between items in the poem.

For example: I crush my wedding glass **beneath** my shoe

Beneath is a preposition.

Write the correct preposition in the following sentences. Sometimes, more than one preposition may be correct. Explain the difference in meaning.

at   by   for   in   on

1. I travel far to find myself _____ home.

2. **a.** I greet a stranger _____ a shopping mall.

   b. I greet a stranger _____ a shopping mall.

   c. I greet a stranger _____ a shopping mall.

2. I take my life and shake it _____ the hair.

3. **a.** I gave him a present _____ his birthday.

   b. I gave him a present _____ his birthday.

4. Let's stay _____ home tonight.

5. **a.** There is a bee _____ your shoe!

   b. There is a bee _____ your shoe!

   c. There is a bee _____ your shoe!

THINK ABOUT IT

1. Why do you think Mr. Reiss wrote this poem?

2. What is your opinion of this poem? Did you enjoy it? Do you understand it? Explain your answer to your class.

3. Is there a poem you like, either in English or in your first language? What is the name of the poem? What is the poem about? Why do you like it?

PART TWO

FO🍴D: **FOOD FOR THOUGHT**

American food is hard to define: Is truly American food hamburgers and hot dogs? Or is it corn, peanuts, and potatoes? Do Americans eat too well, or not well enough? This section focuses on the role food plays in American life, and discusses how certain foods made their way into the American diet.

Before You Read

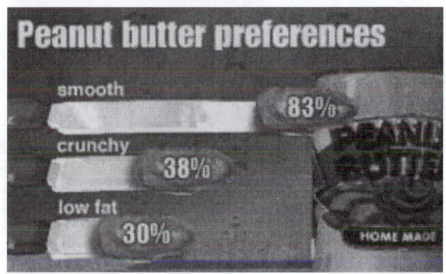

☀USA TODAY Snapshots

Peanut butter preferences

smooth 83%
crunchy 38%
low fat 30%

Smooth or chunky: peanut butter preferences

Nearly 60 percent of Americans of all ages eat peanut butter at least once a week. In the past three months, women ate the following kinds of peanut butter:

    82 percent smooth

    38 percent reduced fat

    36 percent chunky

    30 percent old fashioned or natural

Men liked:

    74 percent smooth

    42 percent chunky

51

40 percent old-fashioned/natural

31 percent reduced fat

The following reading concerns American food—what's popular and why.

Before you read, think about the following questions:
- Do you enjoy American food?
- What kind of food do you think is "typically" American?

Cultural Cues

arroz con pollo Chicken and rice, cooked with mild spices.

Baked Alaska An ice-cream and egg dessert that is baked quickly in the oven.

chow mein A Chinese dish with noodles and vegetables, and sometimes meat.

huevos rancheros Eggs with beans, tortillas, and spicy salsa.

kimchee A spicy cabbage side dish.

lasagne A dish prepared with noodles, tomatoes, cheese, and sometimes meat and vegetables.

pasta primavera "Spring pasta" noodles with vegetables and a light sauce.

polenta A side dish made from ground corn.

ravioli A pasta stuffed with meat or cheese.

scalloped potatoes Potatoes baked with cream and cheese.

sorbet Sweetened, frozen fruit and fruit juice, similar to ice cream.

Steak Diane A particular way of preparing steak.

tagine Meat, sauce, and vegetables or fruit stewed in a covered pot.

WHAT IS AMERICAN FOOD?

Open an American cookbook from the 1960s and you're likely to find recipes for **Baked Alaska** and tuna **casserole**[1]. In the 1970s, it was **Steak Diane** and **scalloped potatoes.** The 1980s brought **pasta primavera** and **quiche**. In the 1990s, it was **polenta** and **sorbet**.

5   Why do food tastes change? One reason may be interest—many people get tired of eating the same food all the time. Another reason might be better transportation. In the past, getting fresh ingredients from another region was difficult. Now, with faster, less expensive transportation, you can enjoy Maine lobsters in Kansas, or Texas beef in Alaska.

10   However, a more important reason might be the changing habits of the American public. They're much more likely to eat out at a restaurant today than they were thirty years ago. With more women working, fewer people cooking, and everyone busier than ever, preparing meals at home is less popular.

15   Thus, food tastes may be changed by the types of restaurant foods people enjoy. Most people who eat dinner out are happy to try something new, or try a new restaurant. And, restaurants, wanting to attract and please their customers, offer a wide and sophisticated selection of dishes.

American cuisine is also influenced by its immigrant population. In the 20   1950s, "ethnic food" usually meant American-style Chinese food, such as chicken **chow mein**, or Italian food, like **ravioli** or **lasagne**. Today, most large cities have wide varieties of restaurants. In San Francisco, you can have **huevos rancheros** for breakfast at a Mexican restaurant, **kimchee** with your Korean lunch, and some Moroccan **tagine** for dinner. In South 25   Florida, Cuban coffee and **arroz con pollo** are popular with all kinds of people, not just Cubans.

So just what is American food? There's no easy answer. However, American food is a wonderful reflection of America: varied, diverse, and always changing!

---

[1]casserole = food baked in a covered dish, usually made of noodles, meat, vegetables, and a sauce.

Check Your Comprehension

1. According to the reading, why do food tastes change? Give three main reasons.

2. According to the reading, why do Americans eat in restaurants more often today?

3. What was "ethnic" food like in the 1950s?

4. How do restaurants influence people's choices of food?

5. What is "American food" according to the author?

 READING

Find out more about **understanding and categorizing** by looking in the Reference Guide to Reading Strategies on pages xii–xiv.

Understanding by Categorizing

In order to organize information in your reading, it may help to **categorize** the information you read.

Start by stating the main idea of the reading in the box, then put the supporting ideas in the circles. You can add more circles or other items to the chart.

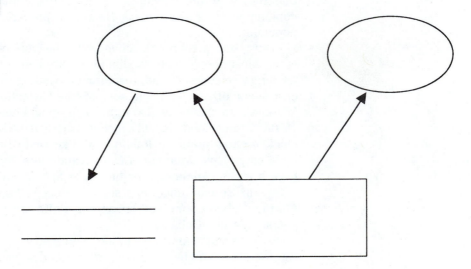

VOCABULARY Food Terms

Look at the following list of words. They were defined for you in Cultural Cues. You will remember them better if you put them into categories. Classify them by answering the questions following the word list.

arroz con pollo	*lobster*	*ravioli*
huevos rancheros	*pasta*	*sorbet*

kimchee   polenta   tagine
lasagne   quiche   tuna casserole

1. things made with eggs: _____

2. things made with pasta: _____

3. things made with corn: _____

4. things made with fish or seafood: _____

5. things made with vegetables: _____

6. things made with fruit: _____

7. things made with rice: _____

8. things you can bake: _____

9. things that are spicy: _____

10. things you eat cold: _____

THINK ABOUT IT

1. What kinds of American food do you enjoy?

2. Which foods from your culture are found in the American diet? Which foods are not? Are there any foods you miss?

3. Do you think the American diet is a healthy one? Why or why not?

Before You Read

Chocolate Chip Cookie Recipe

1 cup butter, softened (2 sticks, ½ pound)

¾ cup granulated sugar (white sugar)

¾ cup brown sugar, packed

1 teaspoon vanilla extract

2 eggs

2¼ cup flour

1 teaspoon baking soda

1 teaspoon salt

2 cups semi-sweet chocolate pieces (12-ounce package)

1. Combine the flour, baking soda, and salt in a small bowl.

2. Beat the butter, granulated sugar, brown sugar, and vanilla in a large mixer bowl.

3. Add the eggs one at a time, beating well after adding each egg. Gradually beat in the flour mixture.

4. Stir in the chocolate pieces. Drop by rounded tablespoons onto ungreased baking sheets.

5. Bake in preheated 375° Fahrenheit oven for 9 to 11 minutes or until golden brown. Let th cookies cool for 2 minutes before you eat them.

The following reading tells about the invention of the chocolate chip cookie.

Before you read, think about these questions:

• Have you ever eaten chocolate chip cookies? Do you like them?

• When do you think the recipe for chocolate chip cookies was invented?

READING

Find out more about **skimming** by looking in the Reference Guide to Reading Strategies on pages xii–xiv.

Skimming

Skimming means reading something quickly to get the main idea. Read the following article quickly to determine the main ideas. Read for only two minutes, then write answers to these questions:

1. What is this article about? _____

_____

_____

2. Who is Ruth Wakefield? _____

_____

_____

3. Who is Andrew Nestlé? _____

_____

_____

Cultural Cues   *Andrew Nestlé* A member of the Nestlé family, famous for Nestlé chocolate.

THE TOLL HOUSE INN : SITE OF AN AMERICAN INVENTION

Have you ever had chocolate chip cookies? You probably have. However, many famous Americans like George Washington, Abraham Lincoln, and Thomas Jefferson never had the chance tp experience this American treat.

The chocolate chip cookie is the most popular kind of cookie in America.
5   Seven billion chocolate chip cookies are eaten every year. In fact, half of the cookies baked in American homes are chocolate chip cookies.

Chocolate chip cookies were invented at the Toll House Inn in Massachusetts. Ruth Wakefield and her husband Kenneth bought the Toll House Inn in 1930. One day, Ruth ran out of baker's chocolate, so she broke up one
10   of the bars of semi-sweet chocolate that **Andrew Nestlé** had given her. She thought that it would mix together with the cookie dough and make an all-chocolate cookie. Needless to say, it didn't. Instead, small pieces of chocolate were baked throughout the cookie. She called the new cookie the "Toll House Cookie."
15   As the Toll House cookie became popular, Nestlé began making their chocolate the same way Ruth made the cookies, in small pieces. Nestlé supplied Ruth with the chocolate she used in her famous cookies.

Ruth and Kenneth sold the Toll House Inn in 1966. The new owners tried to turn it into a nightclub. In 1970, it was sold again. Another family bought
20   it and turned it back into an inn. Ruth Wakefield continued to make the original cookies at a bakery down the road.

Unfortunately, the Toll House burned down on New Year's Eve, 1984. However, Toll House cookies continue to be popular today. Their recipe still appears on packages of Nestlé's chocolate chips.

Check Your Comprehension

1. Why are some cookies called "Toll House" cookies?

2. How did Ms. Wakefield come up with her cookie recipe?

3. Why didn't George Washington eat chocolate chip cookies?

4. What is the connection between Nestlé and Toll House cookies?

5. Can you visit the Toll House Inn today?

VOCABULARY
Chocolate Collocations

A **collocation** is two words that regularly go together. Chocolate has many collocations. Here are 14 of the most common ones.

chocolate eclairs	*chocolate cheesecake*	*chocolate icing (or frosting)*
chocolate mousse	*chocolate cake*	*chocolate milk*
chocolate fudge	*chocolate syrup*	*chocolate chips*
chocolate truffles	*chocolate pudding*	*chocolate bars*
chocolate cookies	*chocolate brownies*	

Which of these collocations do you know the meaning of? With a partner, go through the list and explain what each of them are. For ones you don't know, discuss them with your classmates, or look them up in a dictionary. Describe them here:

1. chocolate eclairs _____

2. chocolate mousse _____

3. chocolate fudge _____

4. chocolate truffles _____

5. chocolate cookies _____

6. chocolate cheesecake _____

7. chocolate cake _____

8. chocolate syrup _____

9. chocolate pudding _____

10. chocolate brownies _____

11. chocolate icing (or frosting) _____

12. chocolate milk _____

13. chocolate chips _____

14. chocolate bars _____

THINK ABOUT IT

 Watch the CNN video about Betty Crocker.

Discuss these questions.

1. Who is Betty Crocker?

2. How was the new picture of Betty Crocker made?

3. How "old" is Betty Crocker?

1. Certain foods, such as the chocolate chip cookie, are thought to be "typically American." What other foods do you think are "typically American"?

2. Do you prefer food store bought or home made cookies? Why?

3. Many people say that they are "addicted" to chocolate. Do you think this is possible? Why or why not? Do you enjoy cooking? Why or why not?

S Y N T H E S I S

Discussion and Debate

1. Many foods are "taboo" or forbidden in different cultures. For example, in the United States, it is taboo to eat horses, dogs, and rats. What foods would you *never* eat?

2. If you had to eat the same three meals every day for the rest of your life, what would they be?

3. Do Americans have a good diet or a poor diet, in your opinion? Why?

4. Weddings and food often go together. What is typically eaten at a wedding in your culture? Is there a special significance to that food?

5. Think about another question to ask your classmates about the ideas in this chapter.

Writing Topics

1. In your journal, write about your opinions of American food. Be sure to use examples to support your ideas.

2. Find out about an American tradition that you don't know much about. Look it up in the library or on the Internet. Write a short report about what you find. Look for this information:
   • The history of the tradition
   • A description of the tradition

3. What food is important to you? Write the recipe, along with how to prepare it on a *recipe card*. Follow this format:

Front of the card:

Name of dish: _____

List of ingredients: _____

_____

_____

_____

_____

_____

_____

_____

_____

Back of the card:

Instructions: _____

_____

_____

_____

_____

_____

_____

_____

_____

On Your Own

1. Special events and food usually go together. Talk to five people and ask them these three questions:

   a. What is your favorite kind of celebration?

   b. Are there special foods or drinks you have for that celebration?

   c. Are there any special traditions?

   Report your answers to your class.

2. Try an American food that you have not tried before. Report to your class on the experience. What kind of food was it? Did you enjoy it?

3. If you can cook, try the recipe for chocolate chip cookies. Bring some to class for your classmates to try.

4. These films feature weddings. Rent one from a video store or borrow it from a library. Give a report to your class:

The Member of the Wedding	*Betsy's Wedding*
My Best Friend's Wedding	*Muriel's Wedding*
The Wedding Singer	*The Wedding Banquet*
Father of the Bride	

★★

A L M A N A C   For additional cultural information, refer to the Almanac on pages 207–222. The Almanac contains lists of useful facts, maps, and other information to enhance your learning.

★★★

CHAPTER 4

People

America is a nation of diverse people with different roles and responsibilities in society. This chapter looks at the characters and accomplishments of two kinds of Americans: American mothers and American heroes.

PART ONE

Heroes: Good Deeds

What is a hero? Who is a typical American hero? This section takes a look at two very different American heroes. One is famous for her bravery during the Civil Rights movement. The other is less famous, but is also heroic for his work to save an endangered animal.

Before You Read

Timeline of Some Important Events in African-American History

Date	Event
1865	The 13th Amendment to the Constitution makes slavery illegal.
1868	The 14th Amendment to the Constitution gives African-Americans equal protection under the law.
1870	The 15th Amendment to the Constitution gives African-American men the right to vote.
1875	The Civil Rights Act gives equal access to public accommodations, such as restaurants and hotels.
December 1, 1955	Rosa Parks refuses to give up her seat on a Montgomery, Alabama bus.
December 5, 1955	Blacks begin a boycott of the bus system in Montgomery.
December 13, 1956	The U.S. Supreme Court outlaws bus segregation.
August 28, 1963	The largest civil rights demonstration ever takes place in Washington, D.C. Martin Luther King Jr. gives a famous speech, "I Have a Dream."
1964	Martin Luther King Jr. wins the Nobel Peace Prize in Norway.
February 21, 1965	Malcolm X is assassinated.
August 6, 1965	The Voting Rights Bill of 1957 becomes law. This law is more powerful than any local laws and practices that prevent minorities from voting.
May 1–October 1, 1967	This is the worst summer for racial problems in U.S. history. More than 40 riots and 100 other disturbances occur.

June 13, 1967	Thurgood Marshall is appointed the first African-American associate justice of the U.S. Supreme Court.
1968	The Civil Rights Act outlaws discrimination in housing.
April 4, 1968	Martin Luther King Jr. is assassinated.
October 29, 1969	U.S. Supreme Court rules that school districts must immediately end racial segregation.

The following reading tells the story of Rosa Parks, a famous American civil rights hero.

Before you read, think about these questions:

- Have you heard of Rosa Parks?
- What do you know about the Civil Rights movement in the United States?

Cultural Cues

Klan   The Ku Klux Klan is an organization that believes in the superiority of white people. It has been responsible for many acts of violence against minorities.

Civil Rights Movement   Political and social activity that began in the 1950s; it fought for the rights of all people to share the same freedoms. Its most famous leader was Martin Luther King, Jr.

lynching   The attack and hanging of a person accused of a crime, without any legal process. In the past lynchings were frequently racially motivated.

Baptist   A type of Christian religion.

NAACP   An organization which exists to encourage the advancement of African Americans.

READING

Find out more about **increasing speed** by looking in the Reference Guide to Reading Strategies on pages xii–xiv.

Increasing Speed

A native English speaker reads at about 250 words per minute. Of course, you probably don't read that quickly. However, reading too slowly can cause you to understand *less* of your reading. For example, you may forget the main idea of a sentence by the time you get to the end. When you read more quickly, you read groups of words at the same time. This gives you a more complete context, so it's easier to guess the meanings of unknown words, too. It's a good idea to try to read at a fairly quick speed.

The reading activity for this chapter focuses on **increasing reading speed.** Mark the time you start reading. Try to read at a comfortable pace, but read as quickly as you can while still understanding the text.

Starting Time: ＿＿:＿＿

☙ ROSA PARKS ❧
A HERO OF CIVIL RIGHTS

Most historians say that the beginning of the modern **civil rights movement** in the United States was December 1, 1955. That was the day when an unknown **seamstress**[1] in Montgomery, Alabama refused to give up her bus seat to a white passenger. This brave woman, Rosa Parks, was arrested and
5   fined for violating a city law. However, her act of **defiance**[2] began a movement that ended the laws that racially **segregated**[3] America. Because of this, she also became an inspiration to freedom-loving people everywhere.

Rosa Parks was born on February 4, 1913 in Tuskegee, Alabama. Her parents, James McCauley, a carpenter, and Leona McCauley, a teacher,
10   named her Rosa Louise McCauley. When she was two, she moved to her grandparents' farm in Alabama with her mother and younger brother, Sylvester. At the age of 11, she became a student at the Montgomery Industrial School for Girls, a private school. The school believed that self-esteem was the key to success. This was consistent with Rosa's mother's advice to "take
15   advantage of the opportunities, no matter how few they were."

[1]seamstress = woman who sews clothing as a career
[2]defiance = strong disobedience
[3]segregated = separated

And the opportunities were few indeed. Mrs. Parks said in an interview:

> Back then, we didn't have any civil rights. It was just a matter of
> survival, of existing from one day to the next. I remember going to sleep
> as a girl hearing the **Klan** ride at night and hearing a **lynching** and
> being afraid the house would burn down.

20

In the same interview, she explained that she felt fearless, because she had always been faced
with fear. This fearlessness gave
25 her the courage to fight her con-
viction during the bus boycott. "I
didn't have any special fear," she
said. "It was more of a relief to
know that I wasn't alone."

30 After attending Alabama State
Teachers College, Rosa settled in
Montgomery, with her husband,
Raymond Parks. The couple
joined the local chapter of the
35 **NAACP** and worked for many
years to improve the conditions
of African-Americans in the segregated South.

The bus incident led to the for-
40 mation of the Montgomery Im-
provement Association. The Association's leader was a young
pastor[4] of the Dexter Avenue
Baptist Church named Dr. Martin Luther King, Jr. They called for a **boycott**[5]
45 of the city-owned bus company. The boycott lasted 382 days and brought
recognition to Mrs. Parks, Dr. King, and their cause. A Supreme Court
decision struck down the Montgomery law under which Mrs. Parks had
been fined, and outlawed racial segregation on public transportation.

After her husband died, Mrs. Parks founded the Rosa and Raymond
50 Parks Institute for Self-Development. The Institute **sponsors**[6] an **annual**[7]
summer program for teenagers called Pathways to Freedom. The young
people tour the country in buses learning the history of their country and
of the civil rights movement.

[4]pastor = leader of a church

[5]boycott = strike, refusal to use or be involved with something

[6]sponsors = people or company that pays for and organizes an event

[7]annual = yearly

Source: From the website of the Academy of Achievement: www.achievement.org

"I do the very best I can to look upon life with optimism and hope and
55 looking forward to a better day, but I don't think there is anything such as complete happiness. It pains me that there is still a lot of Klan activity and racism. I think when you say you're happy, you have everything that you need and everything that you want, and nothing more to wish for. I haven't reached that stage yet."

Finishing Time: _____:_____

Subtract your beginning time from your ending time:

Finishing Time: _____:_____
Starting Time: _____:_____
= _____ minutes

Divide the number *541* by the number of minutes you entered above.

_____

This is your reading speed. How close is it to 250? Read it a second time and see if you can read a little more quickly if you think your rate is too slow. Set a goal for yourself:

Current speed: _____   Goal: _____

Check Your Comprehension

1. What was the law that Rosa Parks broke in 1955?

2. What was important about Rosa Parks' education?

3. What did the African-American community do after Rosa Parks was arrested?

4. How did Mrs. Parks get the courage to fight the law?

5. What was the result of Mrs. Parks' actions?

6. What is "Pathways to Freedom"?

7. Why is Rosa Parks not happy yet?

VOCABULARY
Synonyms

A **synonym** is a word that means nearly the same thing as another word. Draw a line from the word in the first column to its synonym in the second column. The first is done for you as an example.

1. *arrest*	**A.**	appreciation
2. *boycott*	**B.**	apprehension
3. *pastor*	**C.**	break
4. *courage*	**D.**	yearly
5. *recognition*	**E.**	hopefulness
6. *optimism*	**F.**	bravery
7. *segregation*	**G.**	church leader
8. *annual*	**H.**	seamstress
9. *tailor*	**I.**	separation
10. *violate*	**J.**	strike

THINK ABOUT IT

 Watch the CNN video on the Civil Rights Memorial. **Discuss these questions.**

1. Who designed the Civil Rights Memorial?

2. Why is the memorial important?

3. Why are those honored by the memorial heroes?

1. What do you think of Mrs. Parks' actions? Would you have refused to give up your seat?

2. Have you ever boycotted anything? Why?

3. Mrs. Parks broke the law when she refused to give up her seat. Was she right to break the law?

Before You Read

Wild Mustangs

South Dakota

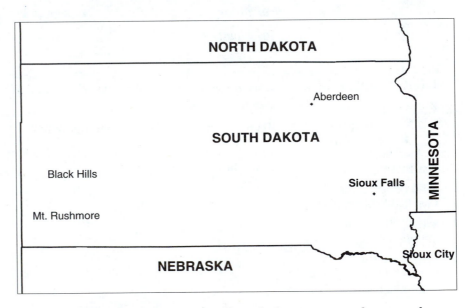

In the following article, you will read about a man who saves horses from extinction. Before you read this piece, think about these questions:

- Did you know that there are wild horses in the western United States?
- Have you ridden a horse?
- Have you ever visited a ranch?

Cultural Cues

pickup truck A popular type of truck used for transporting materials.

Bureau of Land Management A government office that controls public lands.

Mount Rushmore A monument in South Dakota, upon which four Presidents faces are carved: Washington, Lincoln, Jefferson, and Roosevelt.

Born to Run Free

by Randy Fitzgerald

On a **plateau**[1] in South Dakota, a herd of wild horses stands in the sun. Suddenly these **mustangs**[2]—black, white, gray, and pinto—detect an unfamiliar odor. They run until they
5 disappear over the **horizon**[3].

Dayton Hyde leans out the window of his **pickup truck** for a last look at them. "Adding horses to this land was like adding rhythm to music," he says. "They were born to run free."
10 For nine years Hyde, 72, has lived alone on a large ranch watching over hundreds of wild horses. He has also saved them from **extinction**[4]. He has had a long career as a conservationist.

15 Many Americans think that only the government can preserve the environment, including wildlife. However, some individuals like Dayton Hyde rely on private sources. "These property owners care deeply about the land and
20 the wildlife," says Terry Anderson, director of Montana's Political Economy Research Center. "They have discovered that the public, too, will support such private **initiatives**[5], including paying an entrance or user's fee."

25 Hyde was 13 years old when he first saw mustangs on his uncle's Oregon ranch. Many of these wild horses come from herds brought to the New World by the Spanish explorers. They were once a part of huge herds, but by
30 1970 there were only 17,000 because they were captured and used as pet food.

Hyde became a rancher and founder of Operation Stronghold, a group of landowners who create private **wildlife preserves**[6]. On these
35 preserves, wildlife can exist without harming local farms. He wanted to prove that both private land and horses could be protected.

Through the years, Hyde never forgot the wild horses. In 1987, he learned that the U.S.
40 **Bureau of Land Management** was keeping many of them in animal pens. This cost a lot of money for taxpayers. Hundreds were too old, sick, or wild to be taken to live on farms. Hyde knew he could save them.

45 In Washington, D.C., Mr. Hyde argued strongly before the Bureau of Land Management (BLM) and Congress. He felt that the gov-

[1]plateau = hill with a flat top

[2]mustangs = type of wild horse

[3]horizon = where the earth meets the sky

[4]extinction = death of an entire kind of animal.

[5]initiatives = actions taken to solve a difficulty

[6]wildlife preserves = places that protect wildlife from hunting

ernment system was "too often the enemy of wildlife." He worked to move the mustangs
50 from government pens to private land.

"His idea to have them run free was cheaper and more **humane**[7] than what the government was doing," says John Moorhouse, BLM's Montana branch chief.

55   Hyde finally convinced the BLM and started to look through the western states to find good places for the horses. Forty miles south of **Mount Rushmore,** he spotted a plateau where pine trees and streams attract a lot of wildlife.

60   The horses arrived in small groups from government lands in Nevada, Oregon, and Wyoming. Now more than 350 horses roam Hyde's **refuge**[8], admired by 10,000 visitors a year. These visitors help support the ranch with visitor fees. And Hyde, who is still a volunteer, is
65 an example of what one person can do if he really cares.

[8]refuge = protected place

Source: *Reader's Digest*

[7]humane = kind

Check Your Comprehension

1. Who is Dayton Hyde?

2. What are Mr. Hyde's feelings about government's system of animal protection?

3. What's the BLM?

4. How did the government treat the horses?

5. What is "Operation Stronghold"?

6. Who helps pay for the horse refuge?

7. How much does Mr. Hyde get paid for his work?

8. Where do the wild horses come from originally?

 READING

Find out more about **finding the main idea** by looking in the Reference Guide to Reading Strategies on pages xii–xiv.

Finding the Main Idea

Readings usually contain many ideas. Therefore, it's important to understand the **main idea,** in order to understand the importance of the ideas in the story. What do you think the main idea of this story is? Is there more than one? Start by writing a paragraph about what you think the main ideas of this story are. Don't worry about spelling or punctuation.

_____

_____

_____

_____

Review your paragraph. Underline the parts that might be a main idea. Now, write a **one sentence** description of each of the main ideas in this reading.

1. _____

   _____

2. _____

   _____

3. _____

   _____

Compare your answers with a partner's.

VOCABULARY
No Dictionaries!

Look back at the reading for the following words. Write a definition of each word based on your understanding of the word in the reading. Don't use a dictionary!

1. *extinction*

_____

_____

2. *herd*

_____

_____

3. *horizon*

_____

_____

4. *initiative*

_____

_____

5. *mustang*

_____

_____

6. *pine*

_____

_____

7. *pinto*

_____

_____

8. *plateau*

_____

_____

9. *ranch*

_____

_____

10. *rhythm*

_____

_____

11. *volunteer*

_____

_____

12. *wildlife*

_____

_____

THINK ABOUT IT

1. What qualities do you think people admire in Mr. Hyde? Think of all the characteristics that you can.

2. Who can protect the environment better, the government, or private citizens? Why do you think so?

3. Do you think Mr. Hyde is a "typical American"? Why or why not?

PART TWO

Mothers: Mommy Dearest

There's nothing "typically American" about motherhood. But mothers in every culture have different roles and duties. These readings look at different aspects of motherhood in the United States.

Before You Read

Look at the cartoon, then answer these questions:

- Is it complicated to cook for a family? Why?
- Is this cartoon similar to situations in your family? Explain your answer.

The following short stories are taken from *Reader's Digest*. These are stories sent in by the magazine's readers. They present humorous stories about motherhood.

Before you read, think about these questions:
- Do you think it's difficult to be a parent?
- Do you have any funny stories about your mother?

Mothers' Stories

My wife, Donna, is the **spark plug**[1] who makes sure the kids are up on time to eat and then catch the school bus. One day she had an early meeting and left while the rest of us were asleep. By the time the kids and I dragged ourselves out of bed and through our morning routine, we were late. My
5 daughter and son wanted notes for their teachers, excusing their **tardiness**[2]. "Okay," I said, "but what's the reason?" After some discussion we settled on: "Please excuse this lateness. Our power went out early this morning."

—Contributed to "Life In These United States" by William H. Speidel

I had spent the week visiting my sister, and we expected our parents to
10 arrive the next day. Early that morning I awoke to the noise of the vacuum cleaner. My sister was hard at work sweeping, dusting and cleaning windows. "What are you doing?" I asked sleepily, as she shoved a dust-cloth into my hand. "Get to work. Mom and Dad will be here by noon." She raced into the kitchen and began mopping the floor.
15   "The place looks great," I protested. "You cleaned it just before I got here."

   "Yes, but for you the house was sister clean," she replied, never **breaking stride**[3] with her mop. "Now it has to be mother clean!" I started dusting.

—Contributed to "Life In These United States" by Jane C. Sutton

[1]spark plug = a part of a car that helps make the engine start
[2]tardiness = lateness
[3]breaking stride = slowing down

20 While home on a break from medical school, my daughter was so busy she seldom sat down to eat a **balanced meal**[4]. Using all the authority I could **muster**[5], I lectured her on the importance of good nutrition, ending my **tirade**[6] with, "The medical schools should teach our future doctors the importance of a good diet." Hugging me, my daughter responded, "They
25 don't need to teach us that. After all, we do have mothers!"

—Contributed to "Life In These United States" by Phyllis Laxton

---

Check Your Comprehension

1. In the first story, what does the phrase "spark plug" mean? How does it relate to the story?

2. Why were the children in the first story late for school?

3. Why was the woman in the second story cleaning the house?

4. In the second story, what does the writer mean by "mother clean"?

5. In the third story, why is the mother upset with her daughter?

6. How did her daughter answer her?

READING

Find out more about **summarizing** by looking in the Reference Guide to Reading Strategies on pages xii–xiv.

Summarizing

Each of the three stories presents a different "picture" of a mother. Summarize the type of mother that is discussed in each:

1. Type of mother: _____

   _____

2. Type of mother: _____

   _____

3. Type of mother: _____

   _____

---

[4]balanced meal = healthy meal including food from all food groups
[5]muster = gather
[6]tirade = long speech

VOCABULARY
New Words

Complete the following sentences, showing that you understand the meaning of the word in **bold**.

1. My daily **routine** includes _____.

2. I am guilty of **tardiness;** this morning I _____.

3. I couldn't **muster** _____.

4. She started a **tirade** because _____.

5. You can't _____ unless you have **authority**.

6. I ate a **balanced meal** today; I had _____.

THINK ABOUT IT

1. Do you think it is difficult to be a mother? Why or why not?

2. Is your mother like one of the mothers in these stories?

3. Did you enjoy reading these stories? Why or why not?

Before You Read

Mother and daughters

The following reading is a transcript of a news program that was on the radio. In this program, which aired on Mother's Day in 1997, the participants talk about being a mother in the 1990s.

Before you read, think about the following questions:
- Have you ever listened to a radio program in English?
- Do you celebrate Mother's Day? How?

Cultural Cues   *The Union* The United States.

Mother's Day Special

PBS / Wisconsin Public Television

DAVE IVERSON: Good evening and happy Mother's Day weekend. I'm Dave Iverson.

JULIE JOHNSON: And I'm Julie Johnson. Welcome to the second program in our "State of **the Union**" series. Tonight, reports on what it's like to
5   be a mom in the 1990s. And the results of a **landmark**[1] study on mother-hood in America.

IVERSON: The first Mother's Day was officially celebrated in West Virginia back in 1908. The **home front**[2] was different then. Only five percent of all married women worked outside the home. But motherhood wasn't
10   exactly **a bowl of cherries**[3]. In 1908, women were still often segregated. Life expectancy was just 54 if you were white, 38 if you were black. And in 1908, moms couldn't vote. A lot has changed since that first Mother's Day nearly 90 years ago.

JOHNSON: Today, most moms do work outside the home. In fact, 60
15   percent go back before their child is one. So what do women have to say about the state of motherhood today? Well, according to our new national survey, it depends. 81 percent of all women say being a mom is tougher today than it was even 20 or 30 years ago. And 56 percent say today's moms are doing a worse job than their own mothers did.

20 **IVERSON:** But when we asked moms if they were personally satisfied with their lives, the overwhelming Answer was, "**You bet**[4]!"

[1]landmark = important
[2]home front = household
[3]a bowl of cherries = easy, happy
[4]you bet! = yes!

JOHNSON: Yet there was one message that women in our survey sent **loud and clear**[5]. Today's moms feel **pressed for time**[6]. They can't get enough of it.

25 **IVERSON:** So, as more moms than ever before head back to work, how well are we all **adapting**[7]? And why are so many moms still stuck trying to figure it out on their own? National Public Radio's Ray Suarez reports from Boston.

RAY SUAREZ: It's **rush hour**[8]. Women are **hustling**[9] to work. In 1977,
30 we could have opened this program the same way. Women, **giving it their all**[10] on the job, picking up kids at day care and starting their nightside chores amid the children who crave their company. For decades, women have coped with the endless days, letting society **postpone**[11] the hard work of changing the rules. The reason we can do the
35 story in very much the same way in 1997 is simple: Work places haven't changed much. School schedules haven't changed much. And the running of a home hasn't changed much either.
(baby crying)

ROSALIND BARNETT: The philosophy in this country is that, "They're
40 your children. You decided to have them. They're your problem."

REVA KLEIN: You have your children in your 20s and 30s. And build your career in your 20s and 30s. They **coincide**[12].

CONNIE GREEN: Shorter workdays would help. Maybe even being able to work from home, occasionally.

45 **LESLIE CZWAKIEL:** It's too easy to **brush aside**[13] what women say. I think, truly, when men really start making a stink, that something will happen.

---

[5]loud and clear = clear, strong

[6]pressed for time = without enough time to do things

[7]adapting = changing, adjusting to change

[8]rush hour = the time when people are either going to or coming home from work

[9]hustling = hurrying

[10]giving it their all = trying very hard

[11]postpone = put off until later

[12]coincide = happen at the same time

[13]brush aside = ignore

Check Your Comprehension

1. What was life like when the first Mother's Day was celebrated?

2. Are mothers satisfied with their lives today?

3. Why does Mr. Suarez think that things haven't changed much for women?

4. What is America's attitude toward mothers according to Rosalind Barnett?

5. What does Connie Green think would help the lives of American mothers?

 READING

Find out more about **scanning** by looking in the Reference Guide to Reading Strategies on pages xii–xiv.

Scanning

Scanning means looking over a text to gather specific information. Read through the text again and complete this table:

1. How many "State of the Union" programs were there before this one? _____

2. In what year was the first Mother's Day celebrated? _____

3. In what state was the first Mother's Day celebrated? _____

4. What percentage of women worked outside the home in 1908? _____

5. What was the life expectancy for a black woman in 1908? _____

6. In 1997, what percentage of mothers return to work before their children are one year old? _____

7. What percentage of women say it's harder to be a mother today than 20 or 30 years ago? _____

8. What percentage of women think they aren't as good at being mothers as their own mothers? _____

VOCABULARY
Idioms and Colloquial Language

The following words or phrases in bold are found in the reading. Select the sentence that is closest in meaning to the original sentence.

1. The **home front** was different then.
   a. Home life was different than it is now.
   b. The front of the house was different then.
   c. It was different to have a home then.

2. Motherhood wasn't exactly a *bowl of cherries*.

   a. Motherhood was easy.

   b. Motherhood was difficult.

   c. Motherhood wasn't easy or difficult.

3. The overwhelming answer was, "**You bet!**"

   a. Most of them said "yes."

   b. They said "yes" loudly.

   c. Their answer was rude.

4. There was one message that women sent **loud and clear**.

   a. The women spoke loudly when they sent the message.

   b. The women sent one message that was loud.

   c. The women's message was clear and strong.

5. Today's moms feel **pressed for time**.

   a. Mothers today have a lot of time.

   b. Mothers today give up a lot of their time.

   c. Mothers today don't have enough time.

6. Women, **giving it their all** on the job . . .

   a. Women, making their best effort at work . . .

   b. Women, giving to everyone at work . . .

   c. Women, giving up their jobs . . .

7. It's too easy to **brush aside** what women say.

   a. It's convenient to ignore what women say.

   b. We should listen to what women say.

   c. Most people think it's easy to understand what women say.

8. When men really start **making a stink**, something will happen.

   a. When men start to stink, something will happen.

   b. When men start complaining, something will happen.

   c. When men start speaking, something will happen.

THINK ABOUT IT

1. Are mothers' lives more difficult or easier in your country than they are in America? Explain your answer.

2. What does "For decades, women have coped with the endless days, letting society postpone the hard work of changing the rules" mean? Do you agree?

3. Which speaker do you agree with most? Why?

S Y N T H E S I S

Discussion and Debate

1. What qualities does a hero have?

2. These people have been called heroes. Do you know who they are? Do you agree they are heroes? Why or why not?

A	B
Martin Luther King, Jr.	Clint Eastwood
Mother Teresa	Arnold Schwarzenegger
Christopher Columbus	Michael Jordan
John F. Kennedy	Superman

What is the difference between the people in Column A and the people in Column B? Are there different kinds of heroes?

3. Should mothers stay home with their children? Should fathers?

4. Many people think of their parents as heroes. What is a "heroic" parent like?

5. Think of another topic to ask your classmates.

Writing Topics

1. In your journal, write about someone who has been a hero to you. It might be a celebrity, or it might be a family member or friend.

2. Write a short essay giving ideas of how life could be made easier for modern parents.

3. Write an essay in which you compare the role of mothers in the United States and in your own country. You may want to start by making a list of the similarities and the differences.

On Your Own

1. Interview five people. Ask them questions based on the following topics.
   - Who is a hero?
   - Should mothers stay at home with their children?
   Compare your answers to those of your classmates.

2. Watch one of the following movies about mothers. Report on the film to your class.

   The Joy Luck Club   *Mother*
   Little Man Tate   *Terms of Endearment*
   Mommie Dearest   *Throw Momma From the Train*

3. Many television shows focus on the role of mothers. Check your television listings and see if any of these programs are broadcast in

your area. Watch one of them, and make some notes about the mother's character. If you can, watch more than one and compare them.

Leave It to Beaver   *Roseanne*

Grace Under Fire   *Family*

Married with Children   *The Simpsons*

The Donna Reed Show

If you can't watch any of these shows, locate a different program that features a character who is a mother. When you watch the show, think about how the mother is shown. Report on the show you watched to your class.

4. Talk to someone who is a mother (talk to your own mother if you can!). Ask her what it is like. You might ask these questions:
   - What time do you get up in the morning?
   - What chores do you do during the day?
   - How many children do you have?
   - How often do you cook?
   - What do you like best about being a mother?
   - What do you like least about being a mother?

If you are a parent, compare your experience to the experience of the mother you interviewed. Discuss your conversation with your classmates.

★★

A L M A N A C   For additional cultural information, refer to the Almanac on pages 207–222. The Almanac contains lists of useful facts, maps, and other information to enhance your learning.

★★

CHAPTER 5

Geography

The United States is one country, but it has many distinct areas. In this chapter, we look at different parts of America: its heartland and its suburbs.

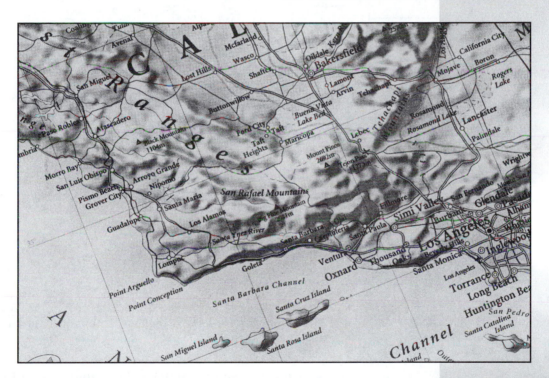

PART ONE

Regions: The Heartland

Each region of the United States has a distinctive character, history, and culture. This section looks at two U.S. regions—the South, whose heart is in Mississippi, and Route 66, an historically important highway that goes right through the heart of America.

Before You Read   A Map of Route 66

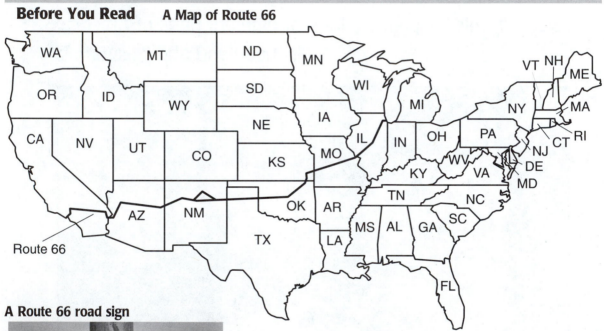

Route 66

A Route 66 road sign

This reading describes an important highway: Route 66. Route 66 was the first American highway to connect the Midwest with the West Coast. This road is so famous, there is even a song about it.

Before you read this article, think about the following questions:

- Have you ever taken a long trip by car?
- Do you prefer to fly or drive when you travel? Why?
- Have you ever heard of Route 66?

Cultural Cues

Mormon A member of a Christian religious group (the Mormons) that originated in the United States.

Will Rogers A humorist, cowboy, and actor born in American Indian territory (now the state of Oklahoma) who was part Native American.

John Steinbeck An American writer whose best-known book was *The Grapes of Wrath* (1939), a story about a poor farming family moving from Oklahoma to find a better life in California.

Okies People who moved from Oklahoma in the 1930s in order to escape drought and poverty.

Woody Guthrie An itinerant folk musician who travelled with his guitar for many years until 1937; his most famous song is "This Land is Your Land".

Merle Haggard A country-western singer who was born in Bakersfield, California.

Dorothea Lange A photographer who is best known for her photographs of poor people taken during the 1930s.

Mickey Mantle A famous baseball player who was born in Oklahoma in 1931.

Jack Kerouac A writer whose most famous book is *On the Road* (1957); it is a story of his travels with several other writers and artists.

About the Author

Michael Wallis was born in Missouri in 1945. He has lived in many different places in the United States, and he has written for many magazines, including *Time*, *Life*, *People*, and *The New York Times*. He lives in Oklahoma.

America's Main Street
by Michael Wallis

Route 66. Just the name is magic.

Route 66. It **conjures**[1] up all kinds of images. *Route 66.* An **artery**[2] linking much of the nation. *Route 66.* An inspiration to literature, music, drama, art, and a nation of dreamers. *Route 66.* A highway fashioned from

[1]conjures = calls, creates a picture
[2]artery = main highway

5 vision and **ingenuity**[3]. *Route 66*. A broken chain of **concrete and asphalt**[4].

Route 66. It has forever meant "going somewhere."

U.S. Route 66, starting at Grant Park in Chicago, reached across more than 2,400 miles, three time zones, and eight states—Illinois, Missouri, Kansas, Oklahoma, Texas, New Mexico, Arizona, California—before it dead-
10 ended at Santa Monica Boulevard and Ocean Avenue in Santa Monica. People like to say the highway started at Lake Michigan and ended in the roaring Pacific. It was one of the country's first continuous spans of paved highway linking East and West.

Almost everyone in the United States, at one time or another, has traveled
15 at least a stretch of its length. One of the most famous highways in the world, parts of it have also been known as the Pontiac Trail, Osage Indian Trail, Wire Road, Postal Highway, Ozark Trail, Grand Canyon Route, National Old Trails Highway, **Mormon** Trail, and the **Will Rogers** Highway. **John Steinbeck** called it "the mother road, the road of flight." Some, like the
20 **Okies,** knew it as the "glory road." Because it went through the center of so many towns, it became the "Main Street of America."

Route 66 is Steinbeck and Will Rogers and **Woody Guthrie** and **Merle Haggard** and **Dorothea Lange** and **Mickey Mantle** and **Jack Kerouac.** It's thousands of waitresses, service station attendants, fry cooks, truckers,
25 **grease monkeys**[5], **hustlers**[6], state cops, **wrecker**[7] drivers, and motel clerks. Route 66 is a soldier **thumbing**[8] home for Christmas; an Okie family still looking for a better life. It's a station wagon filled with kids wanting to know how far it is to Disneyland; a **wailing**[9] ambulance fleeing a wreck on some lonely curve. It's yesterday, today, and tomorrow. Truly a road of
30 **phantoms**[10] and dreams, 66 is the romance of traveling the open highway.

Check Your Comprehension

1. Why does the author think that the name "Route 66" is magic?

2. Where does Route 66 begin and end?

3. How long is Route 66? How many states did it cross?

4. Why is Route 66 called "The Main Street of America"?

[3]ingenuity = cleverness

[4]concrete and asphalt = the materials that roads are made out of

[5]grease monkeys = car mechanics

[6]hustlers = people who make money from gambling, particulary those who cheat or use deception of some kind

[7]wrecker = a truck that takes cars that have been in accidents off the highway

[8]thumbing = hitchhiking

[9]wailing = crying loudly

[10]phantoms = ghosts

5. According to the author, how many Americans have traveled along Route 66? Do you think he's right?

6. What does the author mean when he says "66 is the romance of traveling the open highway"?

READING

Find out more about **finding the main idea** by looking in the Reference Guide to Reading Strategies on pages xii–xiv.

Finding the Main Idea

As you learned in the last chapter, readings usually contain many ideas. Therefore, it's important to understand the **main idea,** in order to understand the importance of the ideas in the story.

This reading contains many examples and descriptions, but they are all used to describe a **main idea.** What is the main idea?

Begin by summarizing the four main paragraphs. What is the point of each of them?

Paragraph 2: _____

Paragraph 4: _____

Paragraph 5: _____

Paragraph 6: _____

Review your summaries. Now, write one sentence that summarizes the **main idea.**

_____

_____

VOCABULARY
Using New Words

This reading introduced many slang terms and new words. Write the correct words from the list in the blanks. You may have to change the form of the words to make the sentences grammatical.

artery	*wrecker*	*hustler*
concrete	*wailing*	*conjure*
grease monkey	*ingenuity*	*thumb (verb)*
phantom	*asphalt*	

1. A _____ cheated my brother out of $100.

2. A slang word for "car mechanics" is _____ .

3. It takes a lot of _____ to build a bridge.

4. Roads are made from _____ and _____ .

5. Route 66 is a _____ of a different, older America.

6. The _____ came after the car accident.

7. A _____ police car drove down the highway.

8. The main _____ through the United States was Route 66.

9. The man _____ a ride to Arizona.

10. The old highway _____ up an image of travel and dreams.

THINK ABOUT IT

1. Why do you think Route 66 has so many different names?

2. Why does the author name so many famous Americans in his description of Route 66? What do they have in common?

3. The author talks about the "romance of the open highway." Do you dream of traveling by road? What do you think it would be like?

Before You Read

A Profile of Tunica, Mississippi

Population	
Today	8,055
1990	8,164
1980	9,652
Education	
Percent high school graduates	45.9
Percent college graduates	8.5
Income	
Average Household Income, 1989	$10,965

Source: U.S. Census

Look at the table. What were the conditions in Tunica, Mississippi around 1990? Answer the following questions:

1. Is the population increasing or decreasing?

2. What is the educational level?

3. How wealthy are the people of Tunica?

Think about your answers as you read the next article, which tells the story of a poor area of the United States. Before you read the article, think about these questions:

• In what part of the United States is the state of Mississippi found?

• What is your opinion of legal gambling?

Cultural Cues

food stamps A federal aid program that gives individuals and families "stamps" with which they can buy food; these are used instead of money at supermarkets.

welfare A government program that provides support for low-income people.

minimum wage The lowest amount a worker can be paid; this amount is set by the government.

MISSISSIPPI MONTE CARLO

by Benjamin Schwarz

In the 1980s, Tunica County, Mississippi, was the poorest county in the poorest state in the country. Life for Tunica's black majority was very difficult. The county had America's 5 lowest average income, eighth highest infant death rate, the fourth highest percentage of births to teenage mothers, and the highest percentage of people living in poverty. In 1984, 70 percent of residents over the age of twenty-10 five had not graduated from high school.

Nearly one-fourth of the houses did not have modern plumbing. There were filthy **shacks**[1] along "Sugar Ditch" Alley, named for the open sewer that ran through it. This image 15 brought in some help from the government, but in 1992 the county was still a symbol of **rural**[2] poverty. Tunica's unemployment levels were among the highest in the state and the country. Even worse, many of those who had 20 jobs did not make enough money to get off **welfare.** That year, more than half the county received **food stamps.**

Ten years ago, the governor hoped that a little industry might come in and employ one or 25 two hundred people in **minimum-wage** jobs.

However, even that seemed very unlikely. Tunica, on an old two-lane road at the northern tip of the Mississippi Delta, was so **isolated**[3], and its population so poorly educated that even 30 state and federal programs could not bring in new business. Although a sign outside the town said that Tunica was "A GOOD PLACE TO LIVE," many parents encouraged their children to leave in order to seek a better life. They felt 35 it was useless to wait for opportunity to come to Tunica.

But that was then. Today Tunica has a future. The highway that residents once took north in search of jobs now has large signs and 40 lights inviting 1.2 million visitors a month into the Delta. In the small town of Robinsonville, a new four-lane road brings drivers west toward the banks of the Mississippi River. Here you will find an Irish castle, a Wild West town, 45 an English mansion, a circus tent, a **plantation**[4] house, a Hollywood studio, and an enormous western **saloon**[5]. These are all casinos. Their signs advertise shows by famous

[1]shacks = small, very cheap houses

[2]rural = country, not the city

[3]isolated = alone, far from other things

[4]plantation = a large farm with many workers. Before the Civil War, plantations in the South had slaves.

[5]saloon = bar, tavern

performers. But just a few feet away, there are still cotton and soybean farms. This gives the area an unreal quality to some people.

"Can you believe this?" one woman asks another, as they wait for a table at a casino restaurant. "Right in the middle of the cotton fields!" she exclaims.

No one dreamed that casino gambling would be a success in Tunica. But this county, which could not attract industry for decades, has turned out to be a perfect location for casinos.

This is partly because Mississippi is eager to welcome gambling. The state doesn't get much in taxes from the casinos, and it charges a casino only $5,000 every two years for a license. Its neighbor, Louisiana charges $100,000 every year. Most other states limit the number of casinos, but Mississippi is like Nevada, the most popular gambling state. It gives an unlimited number of licenses and lets a casino's popularity decide if it will survive. Mississippi's casinos, unlike those in many other states, can offer as many games as they want. And, unlike many states, gamblers can bet large amounts of money if they want.

It may be surprising that it was Tunica's poverty that helped to make casinos so successful. This poverty made Tunicans open to the idea of legalized gambling. Throughout the nation, casinos have become popular in areas that have few other sources of income. Tunica fits this pattern. In 1990, the state authorized casinos along the Mississippi River and the Gulf of Mexico. Tunica was the first county on the river to welcome casinos. "We weren't smarter than other areas," one citizen says. "We were more desperate."

Source: *The Atlantic Monthly*

Check Your Comprehension

1. What was Tunica like in the 1980s?

2. What is responsible for the change in Tunica?

3. How has the Mississippi government attracted gambling to Tunica?

4. Why do some people think the area has an "unreal quality"?

5. Which state is the most popular gambling state?

6. Why is Tunica a "perfect location" for casinos?

7. How did Tunica's poverty make the casinos successful?

 READING

Find out more about **understanding by categorizing** by looking in the Reference Guide to Reading Strategies on pages xii–xiv.

Understanding by Categorizing

Refer to the reading and to the statistics that come before the reading. Fill in the information in the following chart to help you **understand by categorizing.** Use complete sentences.

Tunica in the 1980s

The employment situation _____

_____

_____

The educational situation _____

_____

_____

The family situation _____

_____

_____

VOCABULARY
Words in Context

Use the words from this list to fill in the blanks in the following summary of the first part of the story.

county	*industry*	*sewer*
educated	*isolated*	*shacks*
encouraged	*plumbing*	*stamps*
graduates	*poverty*	*welfare*

In the 1980s, Tunica County, Mississippi, suffered from terrible

_____ . The _____ had America's lowest

average income, eighth highest infant death rate, the fourth highest

percentage of births to teenage mothers. In 1984, seven out of every ten

adults were not high school _____ . Nearly one-fourth of

the houses did not have modern _____ . There were

dirty _____ along "Sugar Ditch" Alley, named for the

_____ that went through it. Many residents who had

jobs did not make enough money to get off _____. That

year, more than half the county received food _____ .

Ten years ago, the governor hoped that a little _____

might come in and employ people. However, Tunica was so _____

_____, and its population so poorly _____

that even government programs could not attract business. Many

parents _____ their children to leave Tunica to seek a

better life.

THINK ABOUT IT

1. In your opinion, are casinos a good solution to poverty? Why or why not?

2. Compare the following statistics about Marin County, California in the 1980s with the information on Tunica in the "Before You Read" section. What differences do you see between Marin County and Tunica County?

Marin County

POPULATION	230,096
RACE	
White	204,646
Black	7,998
EDUCATIONAL LEVEL	
High school graduate	27,848 (12.1 percent)
College degree	62,845 (27.3 percent)
HOUSEHOLD INCOME	
Average household income in 1989	$48,544

Source: U.S. Census

3. Do you think Tunica County might have gotten out of poverty without casinos? How?

PART TWO

TOWNS: MY HOME TOWN

Everyone has different ideas about what makes a good town
or city. The readings in this section focus on what Americans feel about the most
important factors in choosing a place to live.

Before You Read

 Watch the CNN video on the best places to live.

Discuss these questions.

1. Two states have the most "best places to live." Which states are they?

2. What three qualities were considered in the study?

3. What size of city ranked higher?

Would you like to live here? Why or why not?

In this reading, a popular magazine, the *Reader's Digest* asked American families about the best place to raise a family. The magazine reports the results of their survey.

Before you read this article, think about the following questions:

- What does "a good place to raise a family" mean?
- Is your town a good place to raise a family?

Cultural Cues	*light industry* Manufacturing of small items.

About the Author	The magazine *Reader's Digest* is more than 75 years old. It has been a popular source of information, jokes about American life, and condensed versions of articles that appear in other magazines.

The Best Places to Raise a Family

Where is the best place to raise a family? The *Reader's Digest* asked parents across the country about the factors that affect family life. Here are the thirteen factors they found most important:

1. Low crime rate
2. Low alcohol/drug problem
3. Good public schools
4. Quality health care
5. Clean environment
6. Affordable cost of living
7. Strong economic growth
8. **Extracurricular**[1] school activities
9. Access to colleges
10. Many activities for youth
11. Less than one hour to major city
12. Many private schools
13. Warm and sunny weather

Using information about these categories, the *Reader's Digest* asked parents to rate different areas of the United States. Here are the top twenty-five cities:

1. Sheboygan, Wisconsin
2. Kenosha, Wisconsin
3. Fort Collins, Colorado
4. Bremerton, Washington
5. Pittsburgh, Pennsylvania
6. Burlington, Vermont
7. Charlottesville, Virginia
8. Spokane, Washington
9. Boston, Massachusetts
10. Hickory, North Carolina
11. St. Cloud, Minnesota
12. Provo, Utah
13. Steubenville, Ohio
14. Knoxville, Tennessee
15. Ann Arbor, Michigan
16. Glens Falls, New York
17. Dover, Delaware
18. Kankakee, Illinois
19. Bangor, Maine
20. Jackson, Mississippi
21. Galveston, Texas
22. Elkhart, Indiana
23. Monmouth, New Jersey
24. Jacksonville, North Carolina
25. Salinas, California

[1]extracurricular = outside of school, non-academic

The top rated city was Sheboygan, Wisconsin. Here is what the *Reader's Digest* article said about that small town:

Sheboygan, Wisconsin

30   "We consider Sheboygan a secret **haven**[2]," says Ann Scharrer, 39, a mother of four. Just 50 miles north of Milwaukee, it is a secret no longer.

    The town that scored Number One overall got especially high marks for its affordable cost of living and after-school activities. "It's easy to live here, easy to get a job, easy to have someone watch your kid, says Joe Gulig,
35 city editor of the *Sheboygan Press*. Frank Kolenc, 78, explains: "If kids get themselves in trouble, someone is going to see it and tell their parents."

    Sheboyganites may take such an active interest in their children because people put down deep family roots. Many families in town are third- or fourth-generation descendants of German and Dutch immigrants who came
40 in the nineteenth century and stayed. Today, a healthy economy and pleasant life-style keep many young people in the area—2 percent of the population is 20 or younger; 66 percent is under 45.

    Neighborhoods in this city of 51,000 are filled with well-kept homes. Supermarket shoppers leave their car doors unlocked. Children walk home
45 alone after dark from soccer or hockey games. And though Sheboygan faced some difficult economic times in the late '70s and early '80s, unemployment is very small, only 2 percent, thanks to the city's many **light industries.**

Source: *Reader's Digest*

Check Your Comprehension

1. What are the three most important factors in choosing a place to raise a family, according to this article?

2. How many important factors relate to education?

3. Why is Sheboygan so popular with families?

4. What is the history of Sheboygan's families?

5. Why do young people stay in Sheboygan?

[2]haven = calm, peaceful place

READING

Find out more about **summarizing** by looking in the Reference Guide to Reading Strategies on pages xii–xiv.

Summarizing

Reread the article. Make a list of the main points. Then write a letter, **summarizing** the most important points in the article. It can be an informal letter to a friend or family member.

Date:

Dear _____,

I read an interesting article today. It . . .

VOCABULARY
Using New Phrases

These phrases describe the qualities that many Americans look for in a city or town. Complete the sentences showing that you know what these phrases mean.

1. A city with a **low crime rate** would not have many _____

_____ .

2. One feature of **quality health care** is _____ .

3. A **clean environment** includes _____

_____ .

4. For me, **affordable housing** means _____

_____ .

5. One sign of **economic growth** is _____

_____ .

6. My three favorite **extracurricular activities** are _____

_____ .

7. **College access** is important because _____

_____ .

8. A **short commute** is important because _____ .

THINK ABOUT IT

1. Make a list of ten features that you think make a town an enjoyable place to live. How does your list compare to the list in the article?

2. What is your idea of an ideal town (not necessarily in the United States)? Why?

3. Here is some additional information about four of the most popular cities. Look at the information carefully. Which of these would you select? Why?

	Boston	Galveston	Bremerton	Ann Arbor
	Population: 3,240,150 Region: Northeast	Population: 234,688 Region: South	Population: 220,395 Region: West	Population: 515,295 Region: Midwest
WEATHER				
Average July high temperature (Fahrenheit):	81.4	87.6	75.1	83.4
Average January low temperature (Fahrenheit):	22.5	48.3	33.0	17.3
Average annual rainfall (inches):	43.0	42.0	39.0	32.0
Days per year when some rain falls:	128.0	96.0	160.0	133.0
Average annual snowfall (inches):	42.0	0.0	15.0	39.0
ECONOMY				
Median price (3-bedroom home):	$168,500	$110,000	$125,000	$170,000
Recent unemployment rate:	4.1%	7.8%	6.2%	3.2%
CRIME				
Property crimes yearly per 100,000 people:	3,772.8	5,890.3	5,000.0	2,230.0
Violent crimes yearly per 100,000 people:	686.6	1,067.8	300.0	250.0
QUALITY OF LIFE				
Number of doctors per 100,000 people:	388.6	239.8	119.3	200.0
Number of library books per person:	10.7	2.4	1.9	3.8
Number of 4- and 5-star restaurants:	3	2	2	3
Average commute time (minutes):	24.2	23.7	25.1	19.5

Source: *Money Magazine*, "Best Places 1996"

The Simpsons

Before You Read   In the following article, the author talks about a trend in the United States: moving to the suburbs, the neighborhoods outside of cities.

Before you read this article, think about these questions:
- Do you live in the suburbs? Would you like to?
- What are the advantages of living in a city?
- What do you know about the television shows *Roseanne* and *The Simpsons?*

Cultural Cues   *Jeffersonian farmer*   referring to Thomas Jefferson, one of the founders of the United States, who had a large farm.

Gallup Poll   A survey conducted by the Gallup organization, asking citizens their opinions of various issues.

The Adventures of Ozzie and Harriet   A family television show of the 1950s, featuring the real-life family of Ozzie and Harriet Nelson.

Leave It to Beaver   A popular family television show of the 1950s and 1960s.

E.T., the Extra-Terrestrial   A movie featuring a space alien who lives with a suburban family before returning home.

Roseanne   A family television show of the 1980s and 1990s, featuring a lower-middle class family.

The Simpsons   A cartoon popular in the 1990s, featuring the Simpson family, a lower-middle class suburban family.

melting pot   The idea that many cultures come together in the United States to form one culture.

The Suburban Century
by William Schneider

The United States is a nation of suburbs. The 1990 **census**[1] makes it official. Nearly half the country's population now lives in suburbs, up from a quarter in 1950 and a third in 1960.

The third century of American history is shaping up as the suburban
5 century. Until 1920 most Americans lived in rural areas. By 1960 the country was a third urban, a third rural, and a third suburban. That balance didn't last long, however. By 1990 the urban population had slipped to 31 percent and the rural population was down to less than a quarter. We are now a suburban nation with an urban fringe and a rural fringe.

10 The first century of American life was dominated by the rural myth: the sturdy and self-reliant **Jeffersonian farmer.** By the end of the nineteenth century, however, Americans were getting off the farms as fast as they could, to escape the hardship and **brutality**[2] of rural life.

Most of the twentieth century has been dominated by the urban myth:
15 the **melting pot;** New York, New York; the cities as the nation's great engines of prosperity and culture. All the while, however, Americans have been getting out of the cities as soon as they can afford to buy a house and a car. They want to escape the crowding and dangers of urban life. But there is more to it than escape. As Kenneth T. Jackson argues in *Crabgrass*
20 *Frontier,* a history of suburbanization in the United States, the pull factors (cheap housing and the ideal of a suburban "dream house") have been as important as the push factors (population growth and racial prejudice).

The 1990 Census tells the story of the explosive growth of suburbs. That year fourteen states had a majority suburban population, including six of
25 the ten most populous states (California, Pennsylvania, Ohio, Michigan, Florida, and New Jersey).

Suburban growth is not likely to end anytime soon. According to the polls, 43 percent of Boston residents, 48 percent of people who live in Los Angeles, and 60 percent of those who live in New York City say they would
30 leave the city if they could. When the **Gallup Poll** asked Americans in 1989 what kind of place they would like to live in, only 19 percent said a city.

Is there a suburban myth? Sure there is. It has been a **staple**[3] of American popular culture since the 1950s, from television shows like *The Adventures of Ozzie and Harriet* and *Leave It to Beaver* to movies like *E.T.* The

[1]census = count of the population
[2]brutality = meanness, dangerous nature
[3]staple = main part

35 **debunking**[4] of the suburban myth has now reached American popular culture, where television comedies like *Roseanne* and *The Simpsons* portray the harsh realities of suburban life—unemployment, **dysfunctional**[5] families, and, above all, stress.

Source: *The Atlantic Monthly*

Check Your Comprehension

1. Why did people want to escape farms by the end of the nineteenth century?

2. What is the "suburban myth"?

3. Why do Americans want to leave the cities, according to the reading?

4. What does "debunking" mean?

5. How are shows like *Roseanne* and *The Simpsons* different from *Leave it to Beaver* or *The Adventures of Ozzie and Harriet*?

 READING

Find out more about **scanning** by looking in the Reference Guide to Reading Strategies on pages xii–xiv.

Scanning

Look over the article quickly to find the following information. Remember that **scanning** means looking for specific information. So, don't reread the article—just look for these facts:

1. The percentage of Americans who lived in the city in 1990:

   _____

2. The percentage of Americans who lived in the country in 1990:

   _____

3. The percentage of Americans who lived in the suburbs in 1950:

   _____

4. The percentage of Americans who lived in the suburbs in 1960:

   _____

5. The percentage of Americans who lived in the suburbs in 1990:

   _____

6. The percentage of people in 1989 who liked living in the city:

   _____

[4]debunking = showing the truth of something
[5]dysfunctional = not working well, unhealthy

7. The percentage of people in Los Angeles who would like to leave
the city:

_____

8. The number of states whose majority lived in the suburbs in 1990:

_____

VOCABULARY
Using Prepositions

Write the correct preposition in each blank. Review the reading to see how
the prepositions are used. You will use some of these prepositions more
than once.

by   in   of   off   out   to   with

1. _____ 1960 the country was a third urban, a third rural, and
a third suburban.

2. According _____ the polls, 43 percent of Boston residents
say they would leave the city if they could.

3. Americans get _____ of the city when they can buy a house
and a car.

4. By the end of the nineteenth century, Americans were

getting _____ farms.

5. Nearly half the country's population now lives _____ the
suburbs.

6. The Gallup Poll asked Americans _____ 1989 what kind of

place they would like to live _____ .

7. The United States is a nation _____ suburbs.

8. They want to escape the crowding and dangers _____
urban life.

9. We are now a suburban nation _____ an urban fringe and a
rural fringe.

THINK ABOUT IT

1. Do you prefer to live in the city, suburbs, or country? Why?

2. Reread the paragraph explaining the suburban myth. In what ways
does this relate to the idea of the "American Dream"?

3. Why do you think so many Americans say they would like to leave
the city?

S Y N T H E S I S

Discussion and Debate

1. This chapter has offered a lot of information about American regions and areas. What was most surprising to you? Why?

2. Many people argue that "suburbanization" has left the poorest people in the cities, and wealthier people in the suburbs. Is this a problem in your opinion? Why or why not?

3. Can you think of television shows that have made certain parts of the United States famous? (For example, *Dallas* made Texas well-known.) How do those television shows portray those areas? How do they compare to "reality"?

Writing Topics

1. In your journal, write about the town or city in which you are living.

2. Write about a trip you would like to take by car. Where would you stop? Why do you want to go there? Write a short paper explaining your choices.

3. Write a paper in which you compare the advantages of living in a city with the advantages of living in the suburbs. Use many examples.

On Your Own

1. Interview two people who have lived in both the city and in the suburbs. Ask them their opinions about both. You may use these questions, or some of your own:
   - Do you prefer the city or the suburbs?
   - Why?
   - Which city did you live in?
   - Which suburb did you live in?
   - What is one disadvantage of a suburb?
   - What is one disadvantage of a city?

2. Draw a picture and write a paragraph about your ideal fantasy suburb. Include such things as parks, shopping malls, trains to a nearby city, etc. Include whatever would make your suburb a perfect place to live.

3. These films deal with regional topics. Watch one of them and report on it to your class:

The South	**The West**
The Great Santini	*L.A. Story*
The Prince of Tides	*El Norte*
The North	**The Midwest**
Manhattan	*A Thousand Acres*
New York, New York	*The Bridges of Madison County*

4. On the Internet or in the library, look up a city that interests you. Create a short report on the city, and explain to the class why you chose it. Find any maps and photos of the city that you can.

5. Do a research project on legal gambling in the United States. Here is some information you might look for:
   - What states have legalized gambling?
   - Which states have state lotteries?
   - How many people in the United States gamble?
   - How is money from a lottery spent?

   You might look on the Internet or in the library for this information.

★★★

A L M A N A C   For additional cultural information, refer to the Almanac on pages 207–222. The Almanac contains lists of useful facts, maps, and other information to enhance your learning.

★★★

CHAPTER 6

Language

Language keeps people together but it also can keep them apart. There are many controversial issues surrounding the topic of language. What language issues concern you? In this chapter, you will read about language issues affecting the United States.

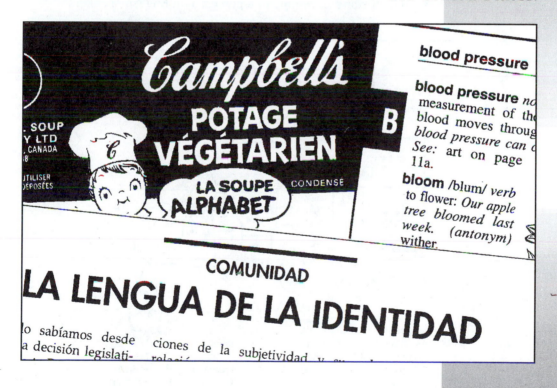

PART ONE

ENGLISH ONLY:
ONE LAND, ONE LANGUAGE

Although the United States has a multicultural population, there are still arguments about the choice of language spoken in the United States. Many people believe that English should be the official language. Others believe that the United States should accept different languages. Where do you stand?

Before You Read

Look at the map and answer the following questions. (Note: The percentage given in each state represent the total percent of non-English speakers in that state.)

- What state has the largest number of languages spoken?
- What state has the largest percentage of non-English speakers?
- Which states have only one percent non-English speakers?

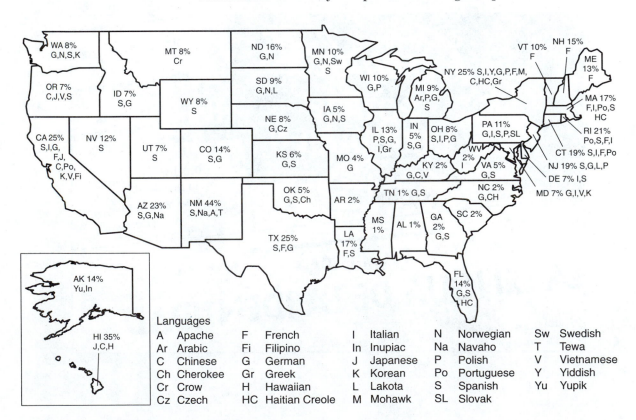

WA 8% G,N,S,K
OR 7% C,J,V,S
ID 7% S,G
MT 8% Cr
WY 8% S
ND 16% G,N
SD 9% G,N,L
MN 10% G,N,Sw,S
WI 10% G,P
MI 9% Ar,P,G,S
NY 25% S,I,Y,G,P,F,M, C,HC,Gr
VT 10% F
NH 15% F
ME 13% F
MA 17% F,I,Po,S HC
RI 21% Po,S,F,I
CT 19% S,I,F,Po
NJ 19% S,G,L,P
DE 7% I,S
MD 7% G,I,V,K
CA 25% S,I,G, F,J, C,Po, K,V,Fi
NV 12% S
UT 7% S
CO 14% S,G
NE 8% G,Cz
IA 5% G,N,S
KS 6% G,S
MO 4% G
IL 13% P,S,G, I,Gr
IN 5% S,G
OH 8% S,I,P,G
PA 11% G,I,S,P,SL
WV 2% I
VA 5% G,S
KY 2% G,C,V
TN 1% G,S
NC 2% G,CH
AZ 23% S,G,Na
NM 44% S,Na,A,T
OK 5% G,S,Ch
AR 2%
MS 1%
AL 1%
GA 2% G,S
SC 2%
TX 25% S,F,G
LA 17% F,S
FL 14% G,S HC
AK 14% Yu,In
HI 35% J,C,H

Languages

A	Apache	F	French	I	Italian	N	Norwegian	Sw	Swedish
Ar	Arabic	Fi	Filipino	In	Inupiac	Na	Navaho	T	Tewa
C	Chinese	G	German	J	Japanese	P	Polish	V	Vietnamese
Ch	Cherokee	Gr	Greek	K	Korean	Po	Portuguese	Y	Yiddish
Cr	Crow	H	Hawaiian	L	Lakota	S	Spanish	Yu	Yupik
Cz	Czech	HC	Haitian Creole	M	Mohawk	SL	Slovak		

In the following reading, the American Civil Liberties Union answers questions about "English Only" laws in the United States.

Before you read this article, think about these questions:
- Does your country have an official language?
- Do you think the United States should make English the official language?

Cultural Cues   *bilingual education programs* Programs in which students are taught in their first language as well as English.

About the Author   The American Civil Liberties Union (ACLU) was founded in 1920 by Roger Baldwin. The ACLU is the United States' leading supporter of individual rights.

"English Only Laws"
by the American Civil Liberties Union

Here are the ACLU's answers to some frequently asked questions about "English Only" laws.

Q: What is an "English Only" law?

5 A: "English Only" laws vary. Some state laws just declare English as the "official" language of the state. Other state and local laws limit or ban the government from giving people help in a language other than English. For 10 example, some restrict **bilingual education programs,** prohibit multilingual **ballots**[1], or forbid any non-English government service. These restrictions include courtroom translation or multilingual emergency police lines.

15 **Q: Who is affected by "English Only" laws?**

A: "English Only" campaigns are mainly against Latinos and Asians, who make up the majority of recent immigrants. Most language 20 minority residents are Spanish-speaking. This is a result of the increase in immigration from Latin America during the mid-1960s.

While the large majority of U.S. residents—96 percent—are fluent in English, approximately ten million residents are not, according to the most recent census.

Q: What kinds of language policies were adopted with regard to past generations of immigrants?

30 A: Our nation was tolerant of linguistic diversity up until the late 1800s. Then, a large number of Eastern and Southern Europeans, as well as Asians, immigrated to the United States. This aroused strong feelings and 35 caused the **enactment**[2] of strict language laws. A 1911 Federal Immigration report falsely argued that the "new" Italian and Eastern Eu-

---

[1]ballots = voting documents

[2]enactment = putting into effect

ropean immigrants were inferior to earlier immigrants, less willing to learn English, and
40 more likely to **betray**[3] the country.

In order to "Americanize" the immigrants and exclude people believed to be of the lower classes, English literacy requirements were established. These applied to public em-
45 ployment, **naturalization**[4], immigration, and voting. The New York State Constitution was changed to exclude over one million **Yiddish**[5]-speaking citizens. The California Constitution was also changed to exclude Chi-
50 nese, who were seen as a threat to the "purity of the ballot box."

Ironically, during the same period, the government wanted to "Americanize" Native American Indian children. They took
55 them from their families and forced them to attend English-language **boarding schools**[6]. There, they were punished for speaking their native languages.

Strong anti-German feelings came with
60 the start of World War I. This caused several states to enact extreme language laws, even though bilingual schools had been common before. For example, Nebraska passed a law in 1919 prohibiting the use of any other lan-
65 guage than English through the eighth grade. The Supreme Court declared the law unconstitutional, however.

Today, as in the past, "English Only" laws in the United States are based on false **stereo-
70 types**[7] of immigrants. These laws do not simply discredit the immigrants' native languages. They attack the rights of the people who speak the languages.

[3]betray = be disloyal to

[4]naturalization = the act of becoming a citizen

[5]Yiddish = an international Jewish language

[6]boarding schools = schools where the students live during the school year

[7]stereotypes = a fixed idea or generalization

**Q: Doesn't bilingual education slow
75 immigrant children's learning of English, in contrast to the "sink or swim" method that was used in the past?**

A: The main purpose of bilingual programs,
80 which use both English and a child's native language to teach all subjects, is to develop English skills. This then makes the child's shift to all-English classes easier. Although arguments about this approach continue,
85 the latest studies show that bilingual education definitely strengthens a child's ability to speak English. Some studies even show that when native language instruction is good, students perform better in all subjects. In ad-
90 dition, the bilingual method brings about self-respect by honoring the child's native language and culture.

The "sink or swim" experience of past immigrants left most of them underwater. In 1911,
95 the U. S. Immigration Service found that 77 percent of Italian, 60 percent of Russian, and 51 percent of German immigrant children were one or more grade levels behind in school. This is compared to only 28 percent
100 of American-born white children. Moreover, those immigrants who did manage to "swim" without help in the past, when farming and factory jobs were plentiful, might not do so well in today's "high-tech" economy.

105 **Q: But won't "English Only" laws speed up the assimilation of today's immigrants into our society and prevent their isolation?**

A: In fact, the vast majority of today's Asian
110 and Latino immigrants are learning English and assimilating as quickly as earlier immigrants did. For example, research studies show that over 95 percent of first generation Mexican-Americans speak English, and that
115 more than 50 percent of second generation Mexican-Americans have lost the ability to speak *Spanish*.

In addition, census statistics show that nearly 90 percent of Latinos five years old 120 or older speak English at home. And 98 percent of Latinos surveyed said they felt it is "essential" that their children learn to read and write English "perfectly." Unfortunately, not enough educational resources are 125 available for immigrants. For example, over 40,000 are on the waiting list for overcrowded adult English classes in Los Angeles.

"English Only" laws do not create new classes to meet these needs. 130 The best insurance against immigrants' social isolation is acceptance—and celebration—of the differences that exist within our ethnically diverse population. The bond that unites our nation is not our similar language 135 or race, but a shared commitment to democracy, liberty, and equality.

Check Your Comprehension

1. What are "English Only" laws?
2. How many U.S. residents are not fluent in English, according to the article?
3. Who is affected by "English Only" laws?
4. What kinds of language policies were adopted in the past in the United States?
5. Why were these old policies enacted?
6. Do bilingual programs slow children's learning of English, according to the article?
7. What is the "sink or swim" method of learning English?
8. According to the article, will "English Only" laws speed up the assimilation of today's immigrants?

 READING

Find out more about **scanning** by looking in the Reference Guide to Reading Strategies on pages xii–xiv.

Scanning

You remember that **scanning** means looking over a text to gather specific information. Quickly read through the text again and complete the table:

Question	Answer
1. How many Mexican Americans cannot speak Spanish?	
2. How many people are on the waiting list for classes in English in Los Angeles?	
3. In 1911, what percentage of German immigrant children were behind in school?	
4. What language do most U.S. language-minority residents speak?	

5. What percentage of first-generation Mexican Americans speak English?

_____

6. What percentage of U.S. residents are fluent in English?

_____

7. What state passed a law in 1919 prohibiting any language but English in elementary school?

_____

8. When did strong anti-German feelings begin in the United States?

_____

9. When did the United States stop being so tolerant of language differences?

_____

10. When was there an increase in immigration from Latin America?

_____

VOCABULARY
Understanding New Words

Review the reading for the words in the first column. If you don't know the meaning of the word, look it up or discuss it with a classmate. Then, write the number of the word in the left column next to the word in the right column that has the closest meaning.

1. *assimilate*   _____ accepting

2. *ballot*   _____ be disloyal to

3. *betray*   _____ become part of

4. *census*   _____ count

5. *discredit*   _____ danger

6. *diverse*   _____ different

7. *enact*   _____ disallow

8. *exclude*   _____ keep out

9. *forbid*   _____ limit

10. *isolate*   _____ make into law

11. *prohibit*   _____ bar

12. *restrict*   _____ put down

13. *stereotype*   _____ keep apart

14. *threat*   _____ fixed image or idea

15. *tolerant*   _____ vote

THINK ABOUT IT

1. How does your experience learning a second language compare to the experience described in the article?

2. Which do you think is more effective: "sink or swim" or bilingual education? Why?

3. In line 52 the article says "Ironically, during the same period, the government wanted to 'Americanize' Native American Indian children." What does this mean? Why is it ironic?

Before You Read

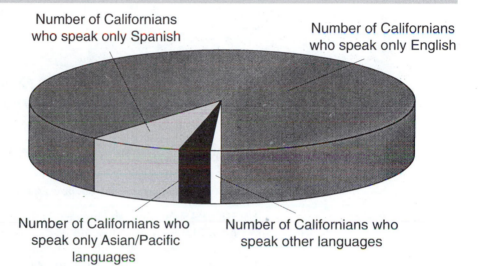

Number of Californians who speak only Spanish

Number of Californians who speak only English

Number of Californians who speak only Asian/Pacific languages

Number of Californians who speak other languages

Calfornians Who Speak Only One Language

Look at the chart and answer these questions:

- What is the most common language in California?
- What is the second most common language in California?

In the following reading, you will read part of a law that was voted on in California in 1998. This law outlawed bilingual education in public schools in California. The law was immediately challenged in court.

Think about these questions before you read:
- Do you think bilingual education is a good idea for children?
- Do you know if other states have outlawed bilingual education?
- Why might someone want to outlaw bilingual education?

Cultural Cues   Because this reading is written in legal language, the writing is different than what you might be used to. The following words are often used in legal documents:

whereas   *Whereas* means *since* or *because.*

thereby   *Thereby* means *therefore.*

About the Authors   Ron K. Unz is a high-technology businessman and the Chairman of One Nation/One California. Gloria Matta Tuchman, an elementary school teacher, is Chair of REBILLED, the Committee to Reform Bi-Lingual Education.

English Language Education for Immigrant Children

*by Ron K. Unz and
Gloria Matta Tuchman*

The People of California find and declare as follows:

(a) **WHEREAS** the English language is the national public language of the United States of America and of the state of California, is spoken by the vast majority of California residents, and is also the leading world language for science, technology, and international business, thereby being the language of economic opportunity; and

(b) WHEREAS immigrant parents are eager to have their children acquire a good knowledge of English, **thereby** allowing them to fully participate in the American Dream of economic and social advancement; and

(c) WHEREAS the government and the public schools of California have a **moral obligation**[1] and a **constitutional duty**[2] to provide all of California's children, regardless of their ethnicity or national origins, with the skills necessary to become productive members of our society, and of these skills, literacy in the English language is among the most important; and

(d) WHEREAS the public schools of California currently do a poor job of educating immigrant children, wasting financial resources on costly

[1]moral obligation = an action that is considered ethically necessary

[2]constitutional duty = the U.S. Constitution requires that all children receive an education

20   experimental language programs whose failure over the past two decades is demonstrated by the current high **drop-out rates**[3] and low English **literacy**[4] levels of many immigrant children; and

(e) WHEREAS young immigrant children can easily acquire full fluency in a new language, such as English, if they are heavily exposed to that language in the classroom at an early age.

25   (f) THEREFORE it is resolved that: all children in California public schools shall be taught English as rapidly and effectively as possible.

Check Your Comprehension

1. Why do the authors believe that English is the language of "economic opportunity"?

2. Why do the authors believe that immigrant parents want their children to speak English?

3. What is the authors' opinion of California public schools?

4. What evidence do the authors supply to support their ideas about California schools?

5. What does this law propose?

READING

Find out more about **understanding fact and opinion** by looking in the Reference Guide to Reading Strategies on pages xii–xiv.

Understanding Fact and Opinion

When you read, it is important to understand the difference between **fact and opinion.** Look at the following statements taken from the reading. Write an *F* by a statement if you think it is a fact and put an *O* if you think it is an opinion. Then, write a short sentence explaining your choice. Discuss your choices with a partner if you like. (You might disagree, which is all right!)

1. _____ The English language is the national public language of the United States of America and of the state of California.

    Explanation: _____

    _____

2. _____ The English language is spoken by the vast majority of California residents.

    Explanation: _____

    _____

[3]drop-out rates = number of students who don't finish high school
[4]literacy = ability to read and write

3. _____ English is the leading world language for science, technology, and international business, thereby being the language of economic opportunity.

   Explanation: _____

   _____

4. _____ Immigrant parents are eager to have their children acquire a good knowledge of English.

   Explanation: _____

   _____

5. _____ The government and the public schools of California have a moral obligation and a constitutional duty to provide all of California's children, regardless of their ethnicity or national origins, with the skills necessary to become productive members of our society.

   Explanation: _____

   _____

6. _____ Literacy in the English language is among the most important skills.

   Explanation: _____

   _____

7. _____ The public schools of California currently do a poor job of educating immigrant children.

   Explanation: _____

   _____

8. _____ The public schools waste financial resources on costly experimental language programs whose failure over the past two decades is demonstrated by the current high drop-out rates and low English literacy levels of many immigrant children.

   Explanation: _____

   _____

9. _____ Young immigrant children can easily acquire full fluency in a new language, such as English, if they are heavily exposed to that language in the classroom at an early age.

   Explanation: _____

   _____

VOCABULARY
Using New Words

The words in **bold** are found in the reading. Please complete the following sentences showing that you understand the meaning of the new words. Reviewing the sentences where these words appear in the reading will help you figure out the meaning.

1. Something that is **costly** _____ .

2. If a school has high **drop-out rates,** _____ .

3. My **ethnicity** is _____ .

4. If you want to reach **fluency,** you must _____ .

5. I believe that parents have a **moral obligation** to _____ .

6. This year, I **resolve** _____ .

7. The _____ is **vast.**

THINK ABOUT IT

1. Do you agree that in America you must speak English to be economically successful? Why or why not?

2. What do you know about bilingual education? Is it a good idea, in your opinion?

3. What is your opinion of the California law you read about?

PART TWO

Regional English: From Sea to Shining Sea

Although "American English" is often talked about as a single language, there are actually many different varieties of American English. From Hawaii to California to Texas to New York, you will find the English spoken in each of these places has its own flavor.

Before You Read

A Language Joke

The number of consonants in the English language is constant. If left out in one place, they show up in another. When a Bostonian "pahks" her "cah," the lost *r*'s migrate southwest, causing a Texan to "warsh" his car and invest in "erl wells."

Read the joke above. Do you understand it? Answer these questions:

• What does "pahk her cah" mean?

• What are "erl wells"?

The next reading talks about a form of language spoken in southern Texas, sometimes called "Spanglish."

Before you read this story, think about the following questions:

• Have you ever been to Texas?

• Do you ever mix your first language with English?

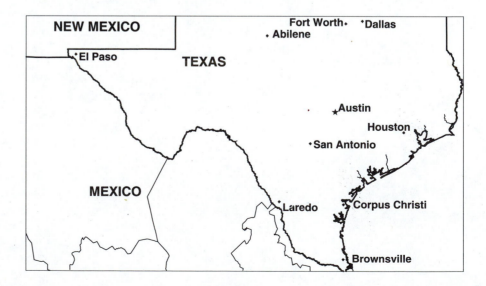

Cultural Cues   ***Tex-Mex*** A short form of the phrase Texan-Mexican; this phrase often describes food, people, and music from southern Texas.

READING

Find out more about **skimming** by looking in the Reference Guide to Reading Strategies on pages xii–xiv.

Skimming

Skimming means reading quickly to get the main idea. Read the next article very quickly—take only three minutes. Then, answer the following questions:

1. What is Spanglish? _____

2. Where is it spoken? _____

3. What does Scott Baird believe? _____

4. What do other researchers believe? _____

Now read the article more carefully.

Lingo or Language ?

by Russell Gold

Professor Scott Baird of Trinity University believes **Tex-Mex,** the blend of Spanish and English spoken in South Texas, is changing into a distinct language.

5 He found his proof in an unexpected place: the graveyard.

Baird, a social linguist, studied the evolution of language on gravestones in **family plots**[1] and found something interesting.
10 Gravestones with a mixture of Spanish and English seem to continue for generations, while earlier immigrant communities, like the Czech and German, gave up their native languages in favor of English within three generations.

15 "The Spanish speakers in large numbers, significant numbers, are going back to the mixed code (of Spanish and English) and hanging on to it, fourth generation, fifth generation, sixth generation," Baird said.

20 He thinks this indicates an unusual occurrence—the beginning of a new language.

The spoken version of Tex-Mex takes English words and adds Spanish **conjugations**[2] but applies English grammatical rules, like
25 word contraction, to a Spanish foundation. For instance, the expression **"to back up"**[3] becomes *"baquear pa'atras."*

Baird's claims that Tex-Mex is a creole, an independent language that neither English nor
30 Spanish speakers can readily understand.

[1]family plots = areas of land in a graveyard in which family members are buried

[2]conjugations = verb endings
[3]to back up = to move backwards or move a car backwards

Most other **linguists**[4] regard it as a dialect of Spanish.

"I'm afraid that Professor Baird is **barking up the wrong tree**[5]," said Mary Ellen Garcia,
35 associate professor of foreign languages at the University of Texas, San Antonio who has studied the Spanish spoken in San Antonio.

"In this case, speakers of Mexican Spanish do understand San Antonio Spanish," she said.

40 Also, Tex-Mex is sometimes viewed as "bad" English or "bad" Spanish. A **stigma**[6] is attached to speaking it, much like Ebonics, or black English.

But Baird said that Tex-Mex, or Spanglish
45 as he prefers, is a complex language that mixes words from English and Spanish. For example, the English "to park" has become "*parquear*," replacing the word in formal Spanish, "*estacionar.*"

---

[4]linguists = researchers who study languages

[5]barking up the wrong tree = looking in the wrong place

[6]stigma = shame, disgrace

Source: *The San Antonio News*

Check Your Comprehension

1. Who is Scott Baird?

2. Why does he believe Spanglish is a language?

3. Where did he find his evidence?

4. What is Mary Ellen Garcia's opinion?

5. What do most linguists believe Spanglish is?

6. Why is there a stigma attached to Spanglish?

**VOCABULARY
No Dictionaries!**

Look back at the text for the words listed here. These words are not defined for you. Without looking at your dictionary, read the paragraphs that contain these words again. Then, write a definition of the word from the context of the reading.

1. *distinct* _____

_____

2. *code* _____

_____

3. *readily* _____

_____

4. *contraction* _____

_____

5. *gravestones* _____

_____

THINK ABOUT IT

1. With whom do you agree, Professor Baird or Professor Garcia?

2. Why do people mix languages, in your opinion?

3. What is your opinion of Professor Baird's idea?

Before You Read

Watch the CNN video on the Gullah Festival.

Discuss these questions.

1. What is Gullah?

2. What is the origin of Gullah?

3. Where is Gullah spoken?

The next reading also talks about a type of language spoken in the United States. However, this one is not a new language, but a very old one.

Before you read, think about these questions:

• Have you ever traveled to an area in the southeastern United States, such as Florida or South Carolina? What was it like?

• Do you know what language the slaves from Africa spoke in the United States?

The Gullah Creole Language

In the southeastern part of the United States is a small piece of land known to linguists as the Gullah Area. This region goes along the coast from Jack-

sonville, North Carolina to Jacksonville, Florida, and includes the sea islands. In this area, there are African-Americans who are **descendants**[1] of the
5 **tribespeople**[2] brought to North and South America during the time of the slave trade. These people still speak types of the old slave language known as Gullah.

This language is called a creole. Gullah came from another type of language, called a pidgin. A pidgin is a language that occurs when two or
10 more languages come into contact. The pidgin that was behind Gullah was spoken by the tribespeople brought from Africa as slaves. Many of the tribespeople were sold into slavery in the West Indies. There, their pidgin language was influenced by the different creoles spoken by the natives in these islands. Later on, plantation owners in the American colonies brought
15 many of the slaves to America. In the United States, the English of the masters on these plantations influenced the pidgin language. Finally, a new language developed. This language, which became known as "Gullah," was learned and used by the second generation of slaves as their native language.

One of the most fascinating features of Gullah is its common use of
20 idioms. Speakers use these meaningful and vivid expressions frequently. They make the language colorful and poetic. However, they also make it somewhat difficult to understand for an average English speaker. But, idioms are useful because they can express complicated thoughts in just a few words. For example:

25 *"Tek'e foot een 'e han"* = to run, or to leave very quickly

"Dry 'long so" = without a reason

"Two-time-one-gun" = a double barreled gun

"Tas'e 'e mout' " = something appetizing to eat

"Lawfully lady" = legally wedded wife

30 *"Haa'dly'kin"* = barely able

According to Virginia Mixson Gerety, who wrote "The Gullah Creole Language," sometimes it takes just one word to express eight different ideas. Then, the speaker uses the same word with a different tone of the voice to form a question, and thus expresses another eight ideas.

35 Although Gullah is related to other languages, it is not a dialect or variety of any other language. Some poeple might think that Gullah is just bad or "broken" English. However, this is not the case. Although it is related to English, it has its own system of grammar, just as other languages do. It also has a sound system and a large vocabulary. However, since this language
40 wasn't meant to be written, there are no rules for spelling.

Gullah is spoken softly, with a smooth rhythm. Since it is English-based, it sounds like English, but you can hear the sounds of the West African

---

[1]descendants = children, grandchildren

[2]tribespeople = people who belong to a group related by language, religion, or custom

coast in it. Although the vocabulary of Gullah is mostly English, it does have a few words from African languages. When you listen to Gullah being
45 spoken, it moght seem like you are hearing African or Jamaican English.

Gullah is not heard much today. The older speakers are dying, and much of the language is lost with them. Cornelia Bailey, of Sapelo Island, writes:

> Our schools are all closed down, our former communities are gone.
> Our churches have only a handful of worshippers left. Our organizations
50 such as the Farmers Alliance, Masonic, Eastern Stars are gone. Why?
> Because the people are all gone.

However, in Charleston, South Carolina, the generations of the past can still be heard. Sound recordings of Gullah and stories written in this language that have captured this nearly forgotten part of America's history. Thus,
55 Gullah accents, words and songs still echo across the sea islands today.

Check Your Comprehension

1. Who are the ancestors of the Gullah people?

2. Explain the history of Gullah briefly.

3. What is a pidgin language?

4. What is a creole language?

5. How many African words are found in Gullah?

6. What is the future of Gullah?

 READING

Find out more about **summarizing** by looking in the Reference Guide to Reading Strategies on pages xii–xiv.

Summarizing

A single paragraph typically has one main idea. **Summarize** each paragraph of the reading in one sentence, showing you understand the main idea. The first one is done for you.

1. There is an area of the United States where there are descendants of slaves who speak a language known as Gullah.

2. _____

3. _____

4. _____

5. _____

6. _____

7. _____

VOCABULARY
Crossword Puzzle

Look at the reading to help find answers to the clues. Write the words in the boxes—one letter in each box.

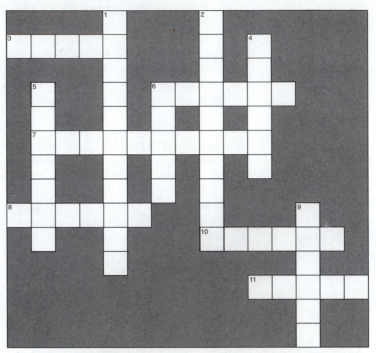

Across

3. A person owned by another
6. A language spoken in the Gullah area
7. A large farm
8. Land surrounded on all sides by water
10. Language of SE coast island
11. A group of people who share a culture

Down

1. Children, or children's children
2. Tasty
4. Land owned by a distant government
5. To state something
6. Shoreline
9. A person born in a specific place

THINK ABOUT IT

1. Do you think there is something special about islands and languages? Explain your answer.

2. Should governments do anything to preserve "endangered languages" like Gullah? What can they do?

3. Is there an interesting language you know about?

S Y N T H E S I S

Discussion and Debate

1. Do you think immigrants should be forced to assimilate into their new culture, or should they have the option to stay immersed in their own culture and language? Why?

2. Are there similarities between the Gullah situation and the Spanglish situation? Explain your answer.

3. With television and film so popular, many people believe that English varieties in the United States will all start to sound the same. Do you think this might happen? Why or why not?

Writing Topics

1. In your journal, write about your feelings about the English language. Has learning it been fun? Has it been difficult?

2. Write a letter to a friend or family member, explaining what you know about varieties of English. If you know about other varieties, not just the ones discussed in this chapter, you can mention those, too.

3. Write an essay in which you defend your opinion about "English Only" laws or bilingual education.

On Your Own

1. Choose an area of the United States whose language interests you. For example, you might choose one of these areas, which have very distinctive language qualities:

   Texas, Boston, the Carolinas, Southern Florida, California

   Do some research in the library or on the Internet about language use in the area you chose. Report to your class on what you found.

2. Talk to an American. (Choose one who is from a different region of the United States if you are living in the United States now.) Ask this person about a regional English spoken in his or her home area. Here are some questions you might ask:
   - Is there a special type of English spoken in your region? What is it called?
   - What words are used that other Americans might not know?
   - What words are pronounced differently?
   - Do you know the origins of that variety of English?

3. Ask five people their opinion on official language policies such as English-Only, or other laws that restrict language use. Ask them if their country has a language policy and if so, how do they feel about that? Report to your class the ideas you find out.

4. Try to find a copy of the video *American Tongues*. It is a documentary about language varieties in the United States. Watch the video and discuss it with your classmates.

★★

A L M A N A C For additional cultural information, refer to the Almanac on pages 207–222. The Almanac contains lists of useful facts, maps, and other information to enhance your learning.

★★

CHAPTER 7

Beliefs

What is important to Americans? Of course, this depends on who you talk to. But it seems most Americans share a belief in democracy and freedom as well as pride in the historic places and monuments that symbolize these beliefs. This chapter looks at some of these beliefs and symbols.

PART ONE

National Symbols: The Red, White, and Blue

Patriotism exists in all countries. Like in many other countries, in the United States, citizens show their patriotism by displaying flags, singing the national anthem, and watching Independence Day parades. The United States also celebrates individual liberty, so many Americans have different ideas of patriotism.

The "Betsy Ross" original American flag with 13 stars

The modern flag with 50 stars

Before You Read

People sometimes criticize the United States' national anthem, or song, because it's a song about war, and it's difficult to sing. Can you understand the words of the song? Work with a partner or small group and rewrite the song in your own words.

Work with one or two lines at a time. Write your understanding of the lines in the blanks on the right. The first four are done for you. Some of the words are defined for you.

The National Anthem: "Star-Spangled Banner"
by Francis Scott Key

Oh, say can you see _____ Can you see _____

by the dawn's early light, _____ early this morning _____

what so proudly we hailed _____ that thing we praised _____

by the twilight's last gleaming, _____ when the sun was setting _____

whose broad stripes and bright stars _____

through the **perilous**[1] fight _____

[1]perilous = dangerous

o'er[2] the **ramparts**[3] we watched ⎯⎯⎯⎯⎯⎯⎯⎯⎯⎯

were so **gallantly**[4] streaming? ⎯⎯⎯⎯⎯⎯⎯⎯⎯⎯

And the rockets' red glare, ⎯⎯⎯⎯⎯⎯⎯⎯⎯⎯

the bombs bursting in air ⎯⎯⎯⎯⎯⎯⎯⎯⎯⎯

gave proof through the night ⎯⎯⎯⎯⎯⎯⎯⎯⎯⎯

that our flag was still there. ⎯⎯⎯⎯⎯⎯⎯⎯⎯⎯

Oh, say does that star-spangled banner yet wave ⎯⎯⎯⎯⎯⎯

⎯⎯⎯⎯⎯⎯⎯⎯⎯⎯⎯⎯⎯⎯⎯⎯⎯⎯⎯

O'er the land of the free ⎯⎯⎯⎯⎯⎯⎯⎯⎯⎯

and the home of the brave? ⎯⎯⎯⎯⎯⎯⎯⎯⎯⎯

The flag is an important symbol for many Americans. It is a visual symbol of liberty and history. In 1976 the U.S. Congress made a law that said how the flag should be treated.

The actual Flag Code is written in legal language. The version that follows has been rewritten in plain English.

Before you read, think about these questions:
- Do you think a flag is an important national symbol?
- Does your country have laws about the flag?
- What does your country's flag look like?

Cultural Cues	***military salute*** A gesture made by placing the hand straight, with the palm down, above the eyebrow.
	stand at attention Standing tall and looking straight ahead without talking.

---

[2]o'er = over
[3]ramparts = defending walls
[4]gallantly = proudly

The  Flag Code

Title 36, U.S.C., Chapter 10

As amended by P.L. 344, 94th Congress

Approved July 7, 1976

170. National Anthem; Star-Spangled Banner

5 The song known as *The Star-Spangled Banner* is the national anthem of the United States of America.

171. Conduct during playing

During the playing of the national anthem when the flag is displayed, everyone except those in uniform should **stand at attention** facing the

10 flag with the right hand over the heart. Men not in uniform should remove their hats with their right hand and hold them at their left shoulders, the hand being over the heart. People in uniform should give the **military salute** at the first note of the anthem and keep this position until the last note. When the flag is not displayed, those present should

15 face toward the music and act in the same manner they would if the flag were displayed there.

172. Pledge of Allegiance to the flag; manner of delivery

The Pledge of **Allegiance**[1] to the Flag, "I pledge allegiance to the Flag of the United States of America, and to the Republic for which it stands,

20 one Nation under God, **indivisible**[2], with liberty and justice for all," should be done by standing at attention facing the flag with the right hand over the heart. When not in uniform, men should remove their hats with their right hand and hold it at their left shoulder, the hand being over the heart. Persons in uniform should remain silent, face the flag, and

25 give the **military salute.**

173. Display and use of flag by civilians[3]; rules and customs; definition

The following rules for the display and use of the flag of the United States of America is established for the use of such civilians or civilian groups or organizations.

[1]allegiance = loyalty
[2]indivisible = not able to be divided or split apart
[3]civilians = people not in the military service

30 **174. Time and occasions for display; hoisting[4] and lowering**

a. It is the universal custom to display the flag only from sunrise to sunset on buildings and on **stationary**[5] flag poles in the open. However, when a patriotic effect is desired, the flag may be displayed twenty-four hours a day if properly lighted during the hours of
35   darkness.

b. The flag should be raised quickly and lowered slowly and with respect.

c. The flag should not be displayed on days when the weather is bad, except when an all-weather flag is displayed.

40 **d.** The flag should be displayed on all days, especially on

New Year's Day—January 1

Inauguration Day—January 20

Lincoln's Birthday—February 12

Washington's Birthday—third Monday in February

45   Easter Sunday—(variable)

Mother's Day—second Sunday in May

Armed Forces Day—third Saturday in May

Memorial Day (half-staff until noon)—last Monday in May

Flag Day—June 14

50   Independence Day—July 4

Labor Day—first Monday in September

Columbus Day—second Monday in October

Navy Day—October 27

Veterans Day—November 11

55   Thanksgiving Day—fourth Thursday in November

Christmas Day—December 25

Other days determined by the President of the United States

Birthdays of States (date of admission)

State holidays

60 **e.** The flag should be displayed daily on or near the main building of every public institution.

f. The flag should be displayed in or near every voting place on election days.

g. The flag should be displayed during school days in or near every
65   schoolhouse.

[4]hoisting = raising

[5]stationary = fixed in one place

Check Your Comprehension

1. Who should remove their hats during the "Star-Spangled Banner?"

2. When should the flag be displayed?

3. When should the flag not be displayed?

4. What does "stand at attention" mean?

5. Can you display the flag at night? Explain your answer.

6. Who should salute the flag?

7. Where should the flag be displayed?

 READING

Find out more about **understanding from context** by looking in the Reference Guide to Reading Strategies on pages xii–xiv.

Understanding from Context

Even though the language of this reading was simplified, some passages might still be difficult to understand. Find the following phrases in the reading. Then, read the words or sentences around that phrase to understand what it means. Write the meanings on the following lines.

1. the Pledge of Allegiance _____

_____

_____

2. the Republic _____

_____

_____

3. the universal custom _____

_____

_____

4. a patriotic effect _____

_____

_____

5. an all-weather flag _____

_____

_____

VOCABULARY
Word Search

This word search includes words about the flag from this reading. First, look up any words you don't know. Then, find the words in the grid and circle them. One is done for you. Remember that words can be found going in any direction. Cross the words off the list when you find them.

anthem	*freedom*	*salute*
banner	~~*military*~~	*star*
blue	*patriot*	*stripe*
display	*red*	*white*
flagpole	*rockets*	

M	O	D	E	E	R	F	E	E	G	Z	U	S	X	D
I	Q	B	I	N	R	E	L	J	B	B	T	K	A	Y
L	V	C	L	S	T	O	I	R	T	A	P	N	N	W
I	J	Q	S	U	P	R	C	D	R	W	N	U	T	E
T	M	V	L	G	E	L	K	K	A	H	C	N	H	P
A	X	A	A	D	Y	O	A	A	E	I	M	L	E	I
R	S	L	T	R	M	D	J	Y	L	T	B	H	M	R
Y	F	W	A	K	M	Q	J	X	K	E	S	V	W	T
T	S	O	J	O	D	V	G	R	R	Y	O	B	N	S

THINK ABOUT IT

1. Why do you think the Congress made laws about the flag?

2. Do you think most Americans obey the flag laws? Why or why not?

3. You notice Mother's Day is on the list of holidays for displaying the flag, but Father's Day is not. What is your opinion of this?

4. Should people be allowed to dishonor the flag—not salute it, or even burn it? (This is a controversial issue in the United States).

Before You Read

The Liberty Bell

In this reading, you will learn about the Liberty Bell, a symbol of American freedom.

Before you read, think about the following questions:
- What symbols do you associate with the United States?
- What objects are symbols of your home country?

Cultural Cues

The Pennsylvania Assembly   A group of representatives that make laws in the state of Pennsylvania.

William Penn   A religious leader and American colonist; he was born in London, England, in 1644. In 1681, King Charles II of England made him the owner of the land north of Maryland. The land was named Pennsylvania for Penn's father. (*Sylvania* means "woods".) Although he is known as the founder of the Pennsylvania colony, he lived there only briefly (1682–1683, 1699–1701). He returned to England in 1701, where he died in the same year.

First Continental Congress   The first national government organization in 1774; the First Continental Congress expressed the country's desire for freedom.

Battle of Lexington and Concord   The first major battle of the Revolutionary War; it took place in two Massachusetts towns on April 19, 1775.

Panama-Pacific Exposition   A world fair and exhibition.

The Liberty Bell

The Liberty Bell changed the world on July 8, 1776, when it rang out from the tower of Independence Hall in Philadelphia. It called citizens to hear the first public reading of the
5 Declaration of Independence.

The Pennsylvania Assembly ordered the Bell from England in 1751 to honor the 50-year anniversary of **William Penn**'s 1701 Charter of Privileges. Penn's **charter**[1], Pennsylvania's
10 original Constitution, tells of the rights and freedoms valued by people the world over. Penn's ideas on religious freedom, Native American rights, and including citizens in the process of making laws were very revolution-
15 ary.

Since the bell was created to honor the Charter's **golden anniversary**,[2] the quotation "Proclaim Liberty throughout all the land unto all the inhabitants thereof," taken from the
20 Bible, was appropriate. The line in the Bible immediately before "proclaim liberty" is, "And **ye**[3] shall **hallow**[4] the fiftieth year." Therefore, the bell celebrated Penn and the 50th year by announcing liberty in the United States.

25 ## The History of the Bell

On November 1, 1751, a letter was sent to London requesting a bell for the State House (now called Independence Hall) **steeple**[5]. The bell arrived in Philadelphia on September 1,
30 1752, but was not hung until March 10, 1753.

It was discovered that the bell was cracked. It had broken either because it was made incorrectly or it was too brittle.

Two Philadelphia foundry workers named
35 John Pass and John Stow were given the cracked bell to be melted down and **recast**[6]. They added an ounce and a half of copper to each pound of the old bell to make the new bell less **brittle**[7].

40 The new bell was raised in the **belfry**[8] on March 29, 1753. However, people in the town thought they added too much copper, and Stow and Pass were asked to try again. Nobody liked the sound of the bell.

45 So, Pass and Stow tried again. They broke up the bell and recast it a second time. On June 11, 1753, the *New York Mercury* reported, "Last Week was raised and fix'd in the Statehouse Steeple, the new great Bell, cast here by Pass
50 and Stow, weighing 2080 lbs."

In November, a state official wrote that he was still unhappy with the bell and ordered a new one from England. When the new bell arrived, people thought that it sounded no bet-
55 ter than the Pass and Stow bell. So the "Liberty Bell" remained where it was in the steeple, and the new bell was placed in the **cupola**[9] on the State House roof and connected to the clock to mark the hours.

60 The Liberty Bell was rung to call the State Assembly into session, and to call people together for special announcements and events. The Liberty Bell tolled frequently. In fact, in

[1]charter = a piece of writing similar to a contract, treaty, or constitution

[2]golden anniversary = 50th anniversary

[3]ye = an old word for *you*

[4]hallow = honor, make holy

[5]steeple = a tall, narrow, pointed part of a bulding, often holding a bell

[6]recast = molded again

[7]brittle = fragile, easily broken

[8]belfry = tower for bells

[9]cupola = dome

1772 a **petition**[10] was sent to the Pennsylvania Assembly stating that the people in the neighborhood of the State House were distressed by the constant ringing of the great Bell.

But, it continued ringing for the **First Continental Congress** in 1774, **the Battle of Lexington and Concord** in 1775, and its most loud tolling was on July 8, 1776, when it called the citizens together to hear the reading of the Declaration of Independence.

In October 1777, the British **occupied**[11] Philadelphia. Weeks earlier all bells, including the Liberty Bell, were removed from the city. It was understood that if the bells were left in place, they would probably be melted down and used for **ammunition**[12] in the war. The Liberty Bell was removed from the city and hidden in the floorboards of a church in Allentown, Pennsylvania.

The Liberty Bell as Symbol

Every picture of the Liberty Bell shows it with a crack. Historians disagree about when the first crack appeared on the Bell. However, eventually it grew so large that it became unringable. The day the discovered they could no

Site of the 1915 Panama-Pacific Exposition in San Francisco

longer ring it was on George Washington's birthday, February 22, 1846.

The crack seemed to have a meaning. The Bell became a national symbol when it was used by the abolitionist movement, the movement to end slavery. It was a very appropriate symbol for a country that was "cracked" and whose freedom was broken for slaves.

More than a **decade**[13] after the Civil War, in the 1880s, the Bell traveled to cities throughout the land "proclaiming liberty" and celebrating the cause of freedom. In 1915, it traveled to the **Panama-Pacific Exposition** in San Francisco.

The Liberty Bell **Pavilion**[14] was opened in 1976 in Philadelphia, in preparation for the nation's **bicentennial**[15] celebrations. Now, on every Fourth of July, the Bell is rung, together with thousands of bells across the nation.

---

[10]petition = a request signed with many names
[11]occupied = Took possession of
[12]ammunition = bullets

[13]decade = ten years
[14]pavilion = an outdoor garden house
[15]bicentennial = two hundred years

**Check Your
Comprehension**

1. Who was William Penn?

2. Why was the Liberty Bell ordered?

3. What was wrong with the first Liberty Bell?

4. How was the Bell fixed?

5. How did the people feel about the second Liberty Bell?

6. Why did some citizens petition the government about the Bell?

7. When did the crack appear in the final Liberty Bell?

8. The Bell has been removed from Pennsylvania twice.
What were the reasons?

9. What did the crack symbolize to some people?

10. How is the Bell used today?

 READING

Find out more about **understanding processes** by looking in the Reference Guide to Reading Strategies on pages xii–xiv.

Understanding Processes

The previous story explains an historical process. This process has many details. It may help you to understand and remember better if you complete a timeline of the information in the reading.

Complete the following timeline to help you **understand processes.** The first event is done for you. Include all the information from the reading.

Date: **Event:**

1751   The Liberty Bell was ordered.

_____   _____

_____   _____

_____   _____

_____   _____

_____   _____

_____   _____

_____   _____

_____   _____

_____   _____

VOCABULARY
New Words

The following words are found in the reading. Review the reading to be sure you know what they mean. Then, fill in the blanks with the correct words or phrases.

belfry	*golden anniversary*	*steeple*
decade	*recast*	*cupola*
proclaim	*brittle*	*petition*
bicentennial	*pavilion*	*toll*

1. A _____ has ten years.

2. A dome might also be called a _____ .

3. A garden area where you might see an exposition is a

   _____ .

4. A narrow, pointed part of a building is called a

   _____ .

5. A place where you would find a bell is a _____ .

6. Another word for "ring" is _____ .

7. If something breaks easily it is probably _____ .

8. If you _____ something, you state it to be true.

9. Something many people might sign in order to express their opinion

   is a _____ .

10. The fiftieth birthday of something is called its _____ .

11. The second hundredth birthday of something is called its

    _____ .

12. To make something out of metal again is to _____ it.

THINK ABOUT IT

1. The quotation on the Liberty Bell says, "Proclaim Liberty throughout all the land unto all the inhabitants thereof." What does this mean? Why is it important to the meaning of the Bell?

2. Do bells have any special meaning in your culture? If so, explain this meaining to your class.

3. Have you ever signed a petition? If so, for what cause?

PART TWO

History: Places of Pride

The United States is a very young nation compared to most other nations of the world. However, Americans have developed a strong sense of pride in both their country and in some special places of historical and symbolic importance in the country. You will read about two of these places, both in Washington, D.C., the nation's capital.

The Iwo Jima Memorial

**READING**

Find out more about **making predictions** by looking in the Reference Guide to Reading Strategies on pages xii–xiv.

Making Predictions

Before you read the story, look at the following:

- The title
- The photograph
- The Cultural Cues

Now, make some **predictions** about the reading. What do you think it will be about? Answer these questions:

1. What does the picture above tell you about the story?

2. What does "Vietnam" refer to?

3. What do you think the story will be about?

Before You Read

This reading describes an important monument in the United States: The Vietnam Memorial wall in Washington, D.C.

Before you read, think about these questions:
- Do you know what a *memorial* is?
- How much do you know about the Vietnam War?
- Have you visited Washington D.C.? If so, what did you see there?

Cultural Glossary

National Mall An area in Washington, D.C. where many monuments and government buildings are found.

Ronald Reagan The 40th President of the United States.

The Vietnam Memorial

Engraving on the Vietnam Memorial:
IN HONOR OF THE MEN AND WOMEN OF THE ARMED FORCES OF THE UNITED STATES WHO SERVED IN THE VIETNAM WAR. THE NAMES OF THOSE WHO GAVE THEIR LIVES AND OF THOSE WHO REMAIN MISSING ARE **INSCRIBED**[1] IN THE ORDER THEY WERE TAKEN FROM US

OUR NATION HONORS THE COURAGE, SACRIFICE AND DEVOTION TO DUTY AND COUNTRY OF ITS VIETNAM VETERANS. THIS MEMORIAL WAS BUILT

---

[1] inscribed = written

The Vietnam Memorial

WITH PRIVATE CONTRIBUTIONS FROM THE AMERICAN PEOPLE. NOVEMBER 11, 1982

The Vietnam Veterans Memorial is the most visited National Park site in Washington, D.C. The Vietnam Veterans Memorial honors the sacrifice of the American military **personnel**[2] during one of the country's least popular wars. By building this memorial, it was hoped that the issue of the personal sacrifice could be separated from the U.S. policy in the war. It was also hoped that the monument would help heal some of the emotional scars left by the war.

Congress authorized the Vietnam Veterans Memorial in 1980, stating that it would be located on the **National Mall** on two acres of Constitution Gardens. Following a contest that had over 1400 entries, a **jury**[3] selected the design of Maya Ying Lin of Athens, Ohio. She was a 21-year old architecture student at Yale University when she won. The black, marble wall that Lin designed drew criticism from many **veterans'**[4] groups because it was so different from traditional war memorials. But, no one wanted the memorial to be controversial, so Frederick Hart's Statue of the Three Servicemen was added to the design. Today, the controversy is gone. The wall is visited by thousands of veterans who come to honor their lost friends and family.

[2]personnel = staff, forces

[3]jury = panel of judges

[4]veterans = people who fought in a war

The Wall was built in 1982 and the Statue of the Three Servicemen was added in 1984. That same year, the Vietnam Veterans Memorial became a National Park at a ceremony attended by President Ronald Reagan. In 1993, the Vietnam Women's Memorial by sculptor Glenna Goodacre was added to represent the work of the women Vietnam veterans.

A total of 57,939 names were originally inscribed on the walls of the memorial in 1982. Since then, as more has been learned about those lost in the war, more names have been added. Currently, there are 58,202 names inscribed in the black marble.

Check Your Comprehension

1. Who is Maya Lin?

2. What does "the names of those who gave their lives and of those who remain missing are inscribed in the order they were taken from us" mean?

3. What were the goals of the monument?

4. Why did some veterans' groups criticize the original design?

5. What additions have been made to the original design?

6. Why do veterans visit the Wall?

VOCABULARY
New Words

Review the reading, looking for the following words. Write the letter from the definition on the right in the correct blank on the left. One is done for you as an example.

___k___	**1.** authorize	**a.** complaint
_____	**2.** ceremony	**b.** conservative
_____	**3.** controversy	**c.** conflict
_____	**4.** criticism	**d.** remembrance
_____	**5.** devotion	**e.** loss
_____	**6.** inscribe	**f.** dedication
_____	**7.** memorial	**g.** ritual
_____	**8.** personnel	**h.** engrave
_____	**9.** sacrifice	**i.** old soldier
_____	**10.** traditional	**j.** staff
_____	**11.** veteran	**k.** approve ✔

THINK ABOUT IT

1. Look at the photos of the Vietnam Memorial and the Iwo Jima Memorial. What is the difference?

2. Do you understand the early controversy over the Vietnam Memorial?

3. Why do you think the Vietnam Memorial has become one of the most popular memorials in the United States?

Before You Read

Millie, Barbara Bush and a friend at the White House

This reading is written from the point of view of a dog—Millie—who was in the White House with the Bush family when George Bush was President. The reading is about the Lincoln Bedroom, which is one of the most historic bedrooms in the White House.

Before you read, think about these questions:

• Have you visited the White House? If so, what was it like?

• What do you think a dog's life is like at the White House?

• Who is the President of the United States now? Does the President's family have a pet?

Cultural Cues

Emancipation Proclamation The act that freed the slaves after the end of the Civil War.

Gettysburg Address A famous speech given by President Abraham Lincoln.

About the Author   Mildred Kerr Bush or "Millie" is the name of Barbara Bush's dog. This dog "wrote" a story about her life in the White House, which became a best-selling book.

The Lincoln Bedroom
by Millie Bush

There are some wonderful beds in the White House on the second floor. I have tried them all. The Lincoln Bedroom has a large carved rosewood bed. All the guests ask for that room, of course. All guests but the President's brothers and sister. Finally, after we had lived in the house for six months,
5 they came to us and asked if they'd be permitted to buy a new mattress for the bed. They said it sagged toward the middle, and did we know it was made of horsehair? I thought it was very comfortable and couldn't understand their attitude. However, since Lincoln never slept in either the bed or the bedroom, the mattress had no historic importance, so the Bushes gladly said yes.

10   Until 1902 the room was an office. It was in this very place that the **Emancipation Proclamation** was signed. As for the bed, it was bought from a Philadelphia **retailer**[1] in 1861 to be used in the principal guest room in the Lincoln White House. History tells us that President and Mrs. Theodore Roosevelt and President Woodrow Wilson did sleep in this beautiful bed.

15   There is a handwritten copy of Lincoln's **Gettysburg Address** on a desk in the Lincoln Bedroom. President Lincoln copied the speech five times to benefit a charity for Civil War soldiers. He signed the fifth and final copy. It is this copy that is in the White House.

Although this is the room where the White House ghost is supposed to
20 appear, the Bushes have not seen it, nor do they believe in ghosts. I must confess that I have not seen one either. I liked hiding my **rawhide**[2] bones in this room, but George followed me down the hall one night and caught me. He said he got tired of buying me new bones and he wanted to know just what I was doing with them. There behind the green curtains he found
25 my **cache**[3]. So, of course, I have now taken to hiding them in couches and chairs all over the second floor.

[1]retailer = shopkeeper, seller
[2]rawhide = leather that has not been tanned
[3]cache = hiding place

Source: *Millie's Book.*
William Morrow & Company

Check Your Comprehension

1. Which of President Bush's guests did not like to sleep in the Lincoln Bedroom? Why not?

2. What is the Bush family's opinion of ghosts?

3. Why wasn't the Lincoln bed considered of historical importance?

4. Why did President Lincoln copy his speech five times?

5. What is the history of the Lincoln Bedroom?

6. Why does Millie like the Lincoln Bedroom?

 **READING**

Find out more about **summarizing** by looking in the Reference Guide to Reading Strategies on pages xii–xiv.

Summarizing

Summarizing can help you better understand what you've read. Reread the story. Then, summarize it in the following space. Don't use any additional space.

_____

_____

_____

_____

Now, compare your summary with a classmate's. Answer these questions:

• What information did you include?

• What did you leave out?

• After reading your partner's summary, would you change yours?

VOCABULARY
Using New Words

Use each of the following words in a sentence, showing that you understand its meaning. If you aren't sure of the meaning, review the reading or look the words up in a dictionary.

1. *sag* _____

2. *attitude* _____

3. *retailer* _____

4. *rawhide* _____

5. *cache* _____

6. *charity* _____

7. *principal* _____

THINK ABOUT IT

1. Why do you think this book was written? Who do you think really wrote it?

2. Would you like to sleep in such an historic bedroom? Why or why not?

3. Have you ever owned a dog? If so, what was he or she (or they) like? If not, would you like to have one? Why or why not?

SYNTHESIS

Discussion and Debate

 Watch the CNN video about First Ladies.

Discuss these questions.

1. Who is Barbara Bush?

2. Who are some famous First Ladies in the United States?

3. How has the first lady's role changed?

1. During the Vietnam War, the United States *drafted* men into military service, that is, young men were forced to serve in the military. Do you agree with this practice? Why or why not?

2. Should people be allowed to burn the flag in protest? Why or why not?

3. What places in your country have national and historical importance?

4. Think of another question to ask your classmates about this chapter.

Writing Topics

1. In your journal, write about your thoughts on patriotism. How important is it to feel patriotic towards your country? What feelings do you have for your own country?

2. In a short essay, write about someone who is your personal hero—not a politician or a movie star, but a friend or family member.

3. Is there an historical event that interests you? Do some research in the library or on the Internet and write a short report about it.

On Your Own

1. Talk to a friend or relative who has been effected by a war. Ask him or her about his experience. Take notes. Write about your conversation.

2. Look for information on the White House or the Vietnam Memorial on the Internet. Give a short report to your class about it. For the White House, see: http://www.whitehouse.gov. For the Vietnam Memorial, you might start with the National Parks Service site: http://www.nps.gov

3. Using the Internet or the library, learn about a war that you would like to know more about.

4. These films deal with the subject of war. Check one of them out of your library or a video store and watch it.

   Born on the Fourth of July

   Coming Home

   Glory

   All's Quiet on the Western Front

   Bridge over the River Kwai

   Gone with the Wind

   Forrest Gump

   Saving Private Ryan

★★

A L M A N A C   For additional cultural information, refer to the Almanac on pages 207–222. The Almanac contains lists of useful facts, maps, and other information to enhance your learning.

★★

CHAPTER 8

Entertainment

The United States is well known for its many popular forms of entertainment. Movies, music, television, and sports all make up part of the American entertainment industry. In this chapter, you will read about two areas of this industry: music and comics.

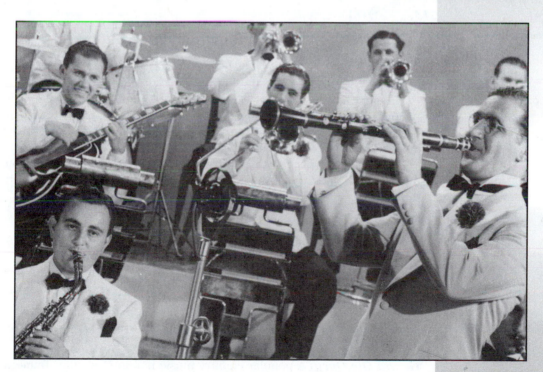

PART ONE

MUSIC: Getting Into the Swing of It

American music has a complex history because of the many different cultures that have contributed to it. They have combined to create a music that is typically American in its many influences.

Before You Read

Five Real Country Song Titles

1. Here's a Quarter, Call Someone Who Cares

2. How Can I Miss You If You Won't Go Away?

3. I Keep Forgetting I Forgot About You

4. If You Don't Believe In Me, I'm Gonna Be Leaving You

5. I've Been Flushed From the Bathroom Of Your Heart

Country music is colorful. Country songs often tell the stories of ordinary people. The musicians that perform country music are often as colorful as the songs they sing. Look at the song titles. Do you understand what they mean? Discuss them with some classmates.

This reading tells the story of one of America's most popular country musicians: Dolly Parton. She is known for her sweet voice and her unique looks.

Before you read, think about these questions:
- Do you know any Dolly Parton songs?
- Do you listen to country music? Do you like it?

Cultural Cues

Greyhound bus A bus that travels long distances. It is an inexpensive way to travel between cities.

Grand Ole Opry A popular country music hall in Nashville, Tennessee.

laundromat A public place to wash clothes.

Dolly Parton

Dolly Parton
by David Arnold

Dolly Parton was the fourth of twelve children. She was born in a cabin near the Little Pigeon River near the tiny town of Locust Ridge, Sevier County, Tennessee. Dolly Rebecca Parton came into the world on January 19th, 1946, and because her family was **dirt poor**,[1] the doctor who delivered

5   her, Robert F. Thomas, was paid with a sack of **corn meal**[2]. Of course, the doctor did not know that Dolly would write a song about him, or that she would become not only a beautiful woman, a multi-millionaire, and a Hollywood star, but perhaps the most famous female country singer of all time.

10   How did Dolly get from Locust Ridge to Hollywood? It was a result of her natural talent and strong determination. A family member recalls "she began singing just about the same time she began talking." She made her first guitar from an old **mandolin**[3] and two extra guitar strings. Even before she went to school, Dolly made up songs and stories and asked her mother

15   to write then down so she could remember them.

[1]dirt poor = very poor
[2]corn meal = ground corn used for cooking
[3]mandolin = a type of musical instrument with four strings

She became a local star at age ten, appearing on a TV show in Knoxville, Tennessee. In 1957, she took a **Greyhound bus** to Lake Charles, Louisiana, where she made her first record, "Puppy Love." A year later, she made her debut at Nashville's **Grand Ole Opry** country music hall, but not as a singer:
20 she played the drums with the Sevier High School Marching Band.

Dolly loved Nashville! However, she was still in high school, so she couldn't go often. She had to work long and hard before graduating in 1964. The day after the graduation ceremony, she fulfilled her first big dream: "I graduated from high school on a Friday night and left early on Saturday
25 morning for Nashville". Her uncle, country star Buck Owens, gave her a place to stay, and on the Saturday she arrived she took a bundle of dirty clothes to the local **laundromat.** There she met Carl Dean, a carpenter. Two years later they were married in Georgia. They are still married today.

Dolly began recording more songs, but none of them became popular.
30 Success finally came to her as a songwriter when another singer recorded "Put It Off Till Tomorrow," and it was **a hit**.[4] Dolly was a fresh and original songwriter, and could find new ways to talk about familiar stories. She sang with a clear, strong, sweet voice. This helped her become popular with
35 people who usually didn't enjoy country music. She also became popular internationally.

In 1967, she began to write lots of popular songs. She appeared on television shows, and received awards for her music, all very quickly. Her looks, personality and sense of humor, made her a natural for the movies. In 1980, she made her movie debut in *Nine to Five*, playing a secretary.
40 Dolly wrote and sang the film's theme song, and it was the most popular song of 1981.

Dolly Parton now owns Dollywood, a large theme park near her hometown; she also bought the local radio station and moved it to Dollywood. She also began a program that promises a college scholarship to every
45 student who graduates from the high schools in her home county.

It's clear why Dolly is still popular after all these years.

Check Your Comprehension

1. How many children were there in Dolly's family?

2. What was Dolly like as a child?

3. How old was Dolly when she started her career?

4. Where did Dolly meet her husband?

5. Why did Dolly become popular with so many people?

6. How does Dolly help her hometown?

[4]a hit = a very popular song

READING

Find out more about **scanning** by looking in the Reference Guide to Reading Strategies on pages xii–xiv.

Scanning

Scanning means reading quickly while looking for specific information. Scan the article quickly and fill out the missing information.

Dolly Parton was the _____ of twelve children. She was born in the state of _____ Her birthday is _____ _____ . The doctor who delivered her was _____ _____ . She became a local star at age _____, appearing on a television show. In _____, she took a Greyhound bus to Louisiana, where she made her first record, "_____ _____ ." A year later, she made her debut at Nashville's _____ country music hall, but not as a singer: she played the _____ . Dolly graduated from high school in _____ . Her uncle, country star _____, gave her a place to stay in Nashville. She met and married her husband, _____ . In _____, she began to write lots of popular songs. In 1980, she made her movie debut in _____, playing a secretary. Dolly Parton now owns _____, a large theme park near her hometown.

VOCABULARY
New Words

Complete these sentences, using your own words and ideas to show that you understand the words and phrases in **bold**.

1. Dollywood is one famous **theme park.**

   _____ is another one.

2. If you were **dirt poor,** you probably couldn't _____ .

3. When you make your **debut,** it's the _____ time that you do something.

4. Dolly's talents made her *a* **natural** for the movies. What are you *a natural* for? _____

5. Locust Ridge is Dolly Parton's **hometown.** What's yours? _____

   _____

THINK ABOUT IT

1. Listen to a Dolly Parton song. Try to understand the words to the song. What is the song about? Did you enjoy the song?

2. Dolly Parton wrote a song about the doctor who delivered her. Who would you write a song about?

3. Here are the words to part of a Dolly Parton song, "Robert". What story is Dolly Parton telling? Write a paragraph that explains the story.

    "ROBERT" by Dolly Parton

      Robert is constantly making eyes at me
      He misunderstands the feelings we share
      There's no way that I can return his glances
5   But I know the meaning of the feeling that's there
      Robert if you knew, there once was a rich boy
      in love with a poor girl long time ago
      But the folks of that rich boy would not let them marry
      And I am a symbol of the love that they stole

10   Oh Robert . . . Oh Robert

      Robert, oh Robert, if you only knew
      The same blood is flowing in both me and you
      That rich boy's your father, but he's also mine
      And my mamma's the poor girl that he left behind

15   Oh Robert . . . Oh Robert

Before You Read

"Heartbreak Hotel"
words & music by Mae B. Axton, Tommy Durden, Elvis Presley

      Well, since my baby left me,
      I found a new place to **dwell**[1].
5   It's down at the end of Lonely Street
      at Heartbreak Hotel.

      You make me so lonely baby,
      I get so lonely,
      I get so lonely I could die.

10   And although it's always crowded,
      you still can find some room.
      Where broken hearted lovers
      do cry away their gloom.

[1]dwell = live

You make me so lonely baby,
15 I get so lonely,
I get so lonely I could die.

Well, the **bellhop's**[2] tears keep flowin',
and the desk clerk's dressed in black.
Well they been so long on Lonely Street

20 They ain't ever gonna look back.
You make me so lonely baby,
I get so lonely,
I get so lonely I could die.

Hey now, if your baby leaves you,
25 and you got a tale to tell.
Just take a walk down Lonely Street
to Heartbreak Hotel.

This reading focuses on a very famous American musician—Elvis Presley.

Before you read this story, think about these questions:

• Have you ever listened to Elvis Presley's music?

• Have you ever seen an Elvis Presley movie?

Watch the CNN video on Elvis Presley.

Discuss these questions

1. What is the name of Elvis Presley's home?

2. Why do so many people visit his home?

3. What did fans think about the marriage of Lisa Presley and Michael Jackson.

Cultural Cues   *rhythm and blues* A type of music that came before rock.

---

[2]bellhop = hotel employee who helps guests with their baggage

Elvisology

Elvis Aaron Presley was born in a two-room house in Tupelo, Mississippi on January 8, 1935. His twin brother, Jessie Garon, died at birth. This left Elvis to grow up as an **only child**[1]. He and his parents moved to Memphis, Tennessee in 1948. Elvis graduated from Humes High School in Memphis
5 in 1953.

Elvis's musical influences were pop and country music, **gospel**[2] music, and the black **rhythm and blues** he heard on historic Beale Street in Memphis. In 1954, he began his singing career at the famous Sun Studio in Memphis. By 1956, he was an international sensation. His sound combined
10 different musical styles and challenged the social and racial barriers of the time. He began a new era of American music and popular culture.

He starred in 33 successful films, made
15 history with his television appearances, and performed many live concerts on tour and in Las Vegas. Globally, he has sold over one billion records, more than other artist. His American sales have earned him more
20 awards than any other artist or group. Even though his stardom might have given him special privileges, he served his country in the U.S. Army.

His talent, good looks, charm, and good
25 humor endeared him to millions of people. Known by his first name, he is regarded as one of the most important cultural figures of the twentieth century. Elvis died at his Memphis home, Graceland, on August 16,
30 1977.

[1]only child = person with no brothers or sisters
[2]gospel = religious

Check Your Comprehension

1. Describe Elvis Presley's family.
2. What was Elvis' music like?
3. How did Elvis' music change American music?
4. How many films did Elvis make?
5. What was Elvis' personality like?
6. What is the name of Elvis' home?

 READING

Find out more about **understanding by categorizing** by looking in the Reference Guide to Reading Strategies on pages xii–xiv.

Understanding by Categorizing

Some readers find that putting information from a reading into a picture or a visual presentation can help them understand the main ideas. Fill in information from the reading in the following chart so that you can **understand by categorizing.** One has been done for you as an example. Add more lines and boxes if you need to.

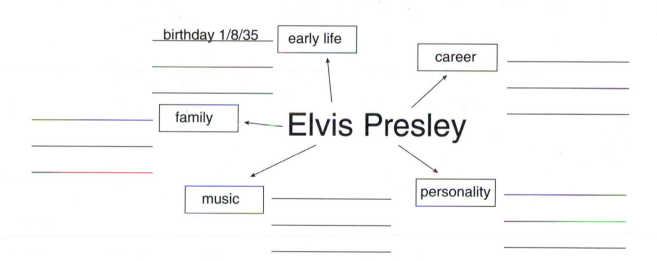

VOCABULARY
Word Meanings

Each word on the left matches one in the column on the right. Draw a line to the correct meaning.

1. *charm*		**a.**	time
2. *era*		**b.**	appeal, allure
3. *gospel*		**c.**	advantages
4. *graduate*		**d.**	Christian; religious
5. *privilege*		**e.**	receive a degree
6. *rhythm*		**f.**	fame
7. *stardom*		**g.**	tempo, beat
8. *tour*		**h.**	double
9. *twin*		**i.**	trip

THINK ABOUT IT

1. Listen to an Elvis Presley song. Try to understand the words to the song. What is the song about? Did you enjoy the song?

2. Why do you think many Americans see Elvis as an "idol"? Why does his popularity continue, in your opinion?

3. Look at the Elvis song at the beginning of this reading. What does it mean? Have you ever heard this song?

PART TWO

Comics: See You in the Funny Papers

Americans love comics. Whether they follow the adventures
of Charlie Brown, or read more sophisticated political cartoons,
Americans enjoy the humor of a wide variety of comics.

Before You Read

The organization of this part of the chapter is a little different from the others. Instead of two readings, you will find some popular cartoons.

Before you look at the cartoons here, think about these questions.
- Do you enjoy reading cartoons?
- Do you read cartoons in English?

 READING

Find out more about **understanding humor** by looking in the Reference Guide to Reading Strategies on pages xii–xiv.

Understanding Humor

Cartoons are, of course, humorous. They also usually contain a min idea. As you read the cartoons, complete the following table to help you **understand the humor.**

Comic	What is the main idea?	Was it funny? Why?
Calvin and Hobbes		
The Far Side		
Dilbert		
Express Lane		

Calvin and Hobbes

Bill Watterson started to draw his popular *Calvin and Hobbes* cartoon in the 1980s. It shows a mischievous boy and his toy tiger. Mr. Watterson no longer draws a daily cartoon strip for the newspapers, but he still occasionally publishes books of *Calvin and Hobbes* comics.

Calvin and Hobbes reprinted by permission of Universal Press Syndicate.

1. What does it mean to "pit your wits" against something?

2. Why don't they catch any fish?

3. What do they decide to eat instead?

VOCABULARY
New Words

If you don't know these words from the cartoon, look them up in your dictionary. Write a definition or draw a picture for each word.

1. *dump* (verb) _____

_____

2. *hook* (noun) _____

_____

3. *net* (noun) _____

_____

4. *sink* (verb) _____

_____

5. *soggy* (adjective) _____

_____

6. *spear* (verb) _____

_____

7. *worm* (noun) _____

_____

About the Cartoonist

The Far Side

Gary Larson's *The Far Side* is known for its clever drawings and silly situations. Gary Larson has stopped drawing *The Far Side*, but collections of his cartoons continue to be published in books.

In an effort to show off, the monster would sometimes stand on his head.

The Far Side reprinted by permission of Universal Press syndicate.

Check Your Comprehension

1. What does "show off" mean?
2. What is the double meaning of "stand on his head" in the first cartoon?

About the Cartoonist

Dilbert

Scott Adams draws Dilbert, a typical office worker in the 1990s. Many workers understand Dilbert's situation and write Scott letters and e-mail messages about their jobs.

Dilbert reprinted by permission of United Feature Syndicate, Inc.

Check Your Comprehension

1. Why does Dilbert (the one with the eyeglasses) have to wait in the hallway?

2. How does the Vice President insult Dilbert?

About the Cartoonist

Express Lane

Brian Orr is a cartoonist who lives in Colorado. He drew this cartoon especially for *Rethinking America.*

| **Check Your Comprehension** | 1. What do you call the woman on the right? |
| | 2. What is the woman on the left doing? Why? |

S Y N T H E S I S

Discussion and Debate

1. What kind of music do you like? Why?

2. What is your favorite form of entertainment?

3. Many people consider reading cartoons a waste of time. Do you agree? Why or why not?

4. Think of another question to ask your classmates about the subjects discussed in this chapter.

Writing Topics

1. In your journal, write about your first memories of music. Here are some ideas to get you started:
   - What is the first song you remember?
   - Did you take music lessons?
   - Did your parents sing to you?

2. Have you ever dreamed of becoming a star? What kind of star would you be? Imagine you are a star, and write a short essay about a typical day in your life.

3. Which of the four cartoons in the chapter did you enjoy most? Write a short letter to a friend or family member recommending this cartoon. Explain why it is enjoyable.

On Your Own

1. Find a radio station that plays music you don't usually listen to. Write down the name of the radio station and the type of music it plays. Did you like the music? Share your experience with your class.

2. Find three people who like music. Ask them who their favorite musician or singer is. Write down your answers and share them with the class.

3. Find a cartoon in a newspaper or magazine that you like. Bring it to class to share and discuss.

4. Go to the library or use the Internet to learn more about one of these topics:
   - The history of rock and roll
   - A biography of a famous musician

   Give a report on what you learned to the class.

5. Draw a cartoon of your own. Create a cartoon with characters and dialogue.

★★

A L M A N A C For additional cultural information, refer to the Almanac on pages 207–222. The Almanac contains lists of useful facts, maps, and other information to enhance your learning.

CHAPTER 9

Technology

Technology is developing at a rapid rate. In the United States, daily life is filled with fax machines, E-mail, cellular phones, and other forms of technology. In this chapter, you will look at two important areas of technology: space exploration and the Internet.

PART ONE

SPACE: Fly Me to the Moon

The exploration of space has been important in America's history. American astronauts have walked on the moon, lived on the Mir space station, and orbited the earth many times in the space shuttle.

Before You Read

Memorable Moments in American Spaceflight

Date	Program	Crew	Duration	Details
May 1961	Mercury–Redstone	Shepard	15 mins.	First American in space
February 1962	Mercury–Atlas 6	Glenn	4 hrs. 55 mins.	First American to **orbit**[1] Earth; 3 orbits
December 1968	Apollo–Saturn 8	Borman, Lovell, Anders	147 hrs.	First orbit of the moon; view of the moon sent to Earth and shown on television
July 1969	Apollo–Saturn 11	Armstrong, Collins, Aldrin	195 hrs. 18 mins.	First moon landing
November 1969	Apollo–Saturn 12	Conrad, Gordon, Bean	244 hrs. 36 mins.	Second moon landing
January 1971	Apollo–Saturn 14	Shepard, Roosa, Mitchell	216 hrs. 1 min.	Third moon landing
August 1971	Apollo–Saturn 15	Scott, Irwin, Worden	265 hrs. 12 mins.	Fourth moon landing, first use of lunar rover
April 1972	Apollo–Saturn 16	Young, Duke, Mattingly	265 hrs. 51 mins.	Fifth moon landing
December 1972	Appollo Saturn 17	Cernan, Evans, Schmitt	301 hrs. 51 mins.	Sixth moon landing
May–December 1973	Skylab 1, 2, 3, 4	Conrad, Kerwin, Weitz, Bean, Garriott, Lousma, Carr, Gibson, Pogue	5,106 hrs.	First U.S. space station
April 1981	Columbia	Young, Crippen	54 hrs. 21 mins.	First space **shuttle**[2] flight

[1]orbit = circle around

[2]shuttle = a reusable spacecraft

Date	Program	Crew	Duration	Details
January 1986	Challenger	Scobee, Smith, Resnik, Onizuka, McNair, Jarvis, McAuliffe	73 secs.	Exploded after takeoff; all seven on board were killed
April 1990	Discovery	McCandless, Sullivan, Shriver, Bolden, Hawley	121 hrs. 16 mins.	Launched the Hubble Space Telescope which sends pictures of space back to Earth
June 1995	Atlantis	Gibson, Precourt, Baker, Harbaugh, Dunbar	269 hrs. 47 mins.	First docking with the Russian space station, **Mir.** The Americans and Russians exchanged crew members.
October 1998	Discovery	Brown, Lindsey, Parazynski, Robinson, Duque, Mukai, Glenn	213 hrs., 44 mins.	John Glenn returned to space as the oldest astronaut to fly a mission

Look at the table and answer these questions:

1. How many times did Americans land on the moon?
2. What is a space shuttle?
3. Which program sent Americans to the moon?
4. What does the Hubble Telescope do?
5. What is "Mir"?
6. What happened to the Challenger?

Cultural Cues

astronauts/cosmonauts People who travel into space. *Astronaut* is the word used for Americans in space, *cosmonaut* is used for Russians.

NASA The National Aeronautics and Space Administration.

the Ritz An expensive hotel in New York, known for its fine service

Cadillac A large, luxury car.

 READING

Find out more about **increasing speed** by looking in the Reference Guide to Reading Strategies on pages xii–xiv.

Increasing Speed

As you learned earlier, reading too slowly can result in understanding *less*, not more, of what you read. Read the next story as quickly as you can. Keep your eyes moving and look at *groups of words*, not individual words; this will help **increase speed.** Mark your starting and ending times on the lines provided here and at the end of the reading.

Starting Time: ____:____

Other Seniors Eager For Space

by Marcia Dunn

NASA's decision to send a 77-year-old John Glenn back into orbit started the space race again, only he contestants were **seniors**[1].

Some of the nation's healthy, older citizens offered to replace Glenn aboard shuttle Discovery in the fall of 1998 as the aging population's repre-
5 sentative in space. At the very least, they wanted to follow in his high-flying footsteps.

"This John Glenn thing brought just a **slew**[2] of requests saying, "How come you picked him? Why not me? I run **triathlons**[3]. Or I do this. Or I do that,'" said David Leestma, director of flight crew operations at Johnson
10 Space Center.

Why not me, demanded an 81-year-old triathlete.

Or me, asked a 77-year-old retired military pilot.

Why not, indeed?

The answer, NASA said, is simple. There's only one John Glenn, a Mercury
15 **astronaut** and former Marine with nearly his entire medical history on file, and he's in **top shape**[4].

"He's been through the whole selection process. We're dealing with a **known commodity**[5]," Leestma explained.

The fact that Glenn was a senator with political connections didn't hurt,
20 NASA insiders admitted.

It had been Glenn's idea, after all, to fly an older person in space.

The former Democratic senator from Ohio and first American to orbit Earth was **intrigued**[6] by the many similarities between aging and the body's changes in weightlessness—weakened bones, depressed **immune system**[7],
25 disturbed sleep. He was so confident both the elderly on Earth and astro-
nauts in space could benefit from space studies that he urged NASA Adminis-
trator Daniel Goldin in 1996 to launch a senior as a medical **guinea pig**[8].

"If I can pass a physical, why not me?" Glenn asked.

[1]seniors = older people
[2]slew = great amount
[3]triathlon = competition in which the contestants compete in three events
[4]top shape = good physical condition
[5]known commodity = familiar product or material
[6]intrigued = fascinated
[7]immune system = the body's defense against illness
[8]guinea pig = person used for a scientific experiment

John Glenn

Glenn easily passed all the necessary medical tests
30 last year. By the time NASA announced his appointment
in January to a nine-day October research flight by
Discovery, he had taken more exams than any other
astronaut candidate.

"He didn't **pull any strings**⁹. He played by the
35 rules and checked out healthy," said Dr. Jerry Lin-
enger, a former Navy physician and astronaut. "He used
to be the **square**¹⁰ guy back in the '60s. He'd go out
and exercise, and didn't drink, and it shows."

Even **hard-nosed**¹¹ Russian space officials were im-
40 pressed with Glenn's health.

"We have **cosmonauts** who have reached their 70s,
but none is in good health," the Russian Space Agency's
chief, Yuri Koptev, said after meeting Glenn. "We envy
you for having older people in such condition."

45   Not everyone was thrilled to have Glenn back in
space.

Some of NASA's 121 astronauts, especially those who hadn't yet flown
in space, resented the fact that Glenn was taking up what could have been
their shuttle seat.

50   The medical testing planned for Glenn in orbit also was called into
question: What good is one scientific subject? And how can such a remark-
ably fit man represent the average 77-year-old?

"I wish we could send up 150 77-year-olds all at one time, right now, and
55 get a database," said Glenn. "Well, we can't do that obviously. Maybe there
will be more later on."

"I don't look at this as **a one-shot deal**¹²," he added.

Leestma said he has no idea how or where he would recruit 70-something
astronauts if instructed to do so. Moreover, he wouldn't necessarily want
to.

60   "In general, space flight is a younger person's game," said Leestma, a
former astronaut. "It's not **the Ritz.** It's not driving your **Cadillac** around.
It's not always easy, you know, and there's a lot of stress. There's a lot of
travel. There are a lot of things involved, especially with the international
space station."

65   No one older than 45 had ever been chosen by NASA as a full-time
astronaut.

And no one older than 61 had ever flown in space.

⁹pull strings = use one's influence

¹⁰square = clean-cut; someone who doesn't drink, smoke, swear, and so forth is "square"

¹¹hard-nosed = tough

¹²one-shot deal = one-time opportunity

That didn't stop 12 people 60-and-up from applying in 1997 for NASA's newest astronaut class, including a pair of 77-year-olds who met the medical qualifications. The 12 were among 2,621 applicants, representing less than one-half of 1 percent.

70

Ending Time: _____:_____

The average English speaker reads about 250 words a minute. How fast do you read? Work out this math:

691 divided by _____ (the number of minutes it took to read the article) = _____ words per minute.

Set a goal for your next timed reading: _____ words per minute.

Check Your Comprehension

1. Who is John Glenn?

2. When did John Glenn first go into space?

3. Why was John Glenn chosen to go into space again?

4. Why were some astronauts upset about Glenn going into space?

5. What do scientists think they can learn from Senator Glenn's trip?

6. How old is the oldest person to go into space?

7. What do the Russians think of John Glenn?

VOCABULARY
Idioms

The following idioms in bold are found in the reading. Review the reading. Then, with a partner, see if you know what all of the idioms mean. Complete each sentence, showing you understand the meaning of the idioms.

1. A **guinea pig** is a person who _____ .

2. A **hard-nosed** person is _____ .

3. _____ was a **one-shot deal.**

4. You need to **pull strings** if _____ .

5. A **square guy** wouldn't _____ .

6. I have a **slew** of _____ .

THINK ABOUT IT

 Watch the CNN video on Space Day.

Discuss these questions with your class.

1. What is Space Day?
2. What kinds of activities happen?
3. What is the purpose of the event?

1. Would you enjoy space travel? Why or why not?
2. Space travel costs billions of dollars. Is it worth it? Why or why not?
3. Do you think older people should be sent to space?
4. Imagine you are going to live on a space colony. You will be gone for a year. Because of weight limits, you may bring only the following items:

> five cassette tapes or CDs
>
> three books
>
> five kilograms of your favorite food (other food will be provided)
>
> one videotape

What will you bring? Which books? Which videotape? Compare your answers with a classmate's.

Before You Read

The first moon landing, 1969

Before you read, think about these questions:
* Would you like to visit the moon?
* What do you know about the moon?

Cultural Cues   *Cape Canaveral* A place in Florida used to launch space vehicles.

Mission to the Moon

A half-moon glowed in the night sky last Tuesday as a **sleek**[1] white rocket blasted off from **Cape Canaveral,** Florida. A small spacecraft called Lunar Prospector was tucked in
5 the rocket's nose. As the rocket rose, people cheered the perfect launch. "We're on our way!" cried one scientist. Soon Prospector broke free from the rocket and began to coast toward the shining moon.
10   For the first time since 1972, the U.S. space agency NASA has launched a mission to the moon. If all goes well, Prospector, which carries no astronauts, will spend one year orbiting the moon. It will map the deeply **cratered**[2]
15 surface. It will find out what the moon is made of and investigate the exciting chance that there is water there.
     Says program scientist Joseph Boyce, who worked on NASA's 1972 moon trip: "It feels
20 good to be going back."

Shooting For The Moon

Humans have always been fascinated by the moon. For centuries we have tracked the passage of time by watching the moon change
25 shape—from new moon to crescent to full moon and back again. We have marveled at man-in-the-moon shadows that lunar cliffs cast over flat plains.

During the 1950s and 1960s, the United
30 States and the Soviet Union raced to get to the moon. Soviet rockets got there first, but the U.S. Apollo program landed the first human there: Neil Armstrong in 1969.
     Americans were thrilled by the discoveries.
35 By 1972, 12 astronauts had walked on the moon, and brought back 850 pounds of rocks. But the United States could no longer afford NASA's expensive missions.
     For the next two decades, our only glimpses
40 of the moon were from telescopes or spacecraft that flew by on their way to other planets. Less than a quarter of the moon has been mapped in detail.

How The Lunar Prospector Works

45 After launch, a wide swing around earth put Prospector on the right path to the moon. Once it's in position orbiting the moon, it will measure the moon's gravity and **magnetism**[3]. Prospector will also look for minerals, gas, and
50 signs of water.

What Will Prospector Find?

Though Prospector won't land on the moon, scientists compare its mission to Pathfinder's thrilling trip to Mars last summer. Both ships
55 were built under NASA's new guidelines: "faster, cheaper, better." The missions are, says

---

[1]sleek = smooth and shiny
[2]cratered = marked with large holes

[3]magnetism = amount of pull or attraction

Boyce, "the start of the next golden age of exploration."

Prospector is less than half the weight of
60 an average car. The spacecraft carries no computer or camera. But it is well equipped for its mission. From 60 miles above the moon, five instruments on the arms and antenna will put together the most complete picture ever of the
65 moon.

Eventually, Prospector will crash-land on the lunar surface, joining the trash and equipment left behind by astronauts. By then, scientists should know a lot more about the moon.

70 ### Will People Live On The Moon?

Some **astronomers**[4] believe that the moon holds as much as a billion tons of ice left long ago by crashing comets. Comets are big, dirty snowballs—mixtures of dust and ice. Most of
75 the ice would have melted, but some may be trapped in areas where the sun doesn't shine.

[1]astronomers = people who study the planets and stars

Recently, scientists found more evidence for this theory. In 1994 the U.S. military launched the spacecraft Clementine to conduct
80 tests near the moon. It spotted what might be a patch of ice at the moon's south pole. If Prospector does find ice, it would look more like icy dirt. "Don't expect to see lunar penguins skating around on a lake!" says Boyce. But ice
85 on the moon could provide water so that astronauts, and maybe ordinary citizens, could live there someday. Scientists would love to set up telescopes on the moon. The views would be outstanding.

90 An air supply would also be needed. But with the right equipment, people can live in strange places. "We have a year-round base in Antarctica," says Boyce. "Today's kids may end up living on the moon."

Source: *Time for Kids*. Time, Inc.

Check Your Comprehension

1. Why did the United States stop sending spaceships to the moon?

2. Why is the United States returning to the moon?

3. How big is Prospector?

4. Why were Russia and the United States in competition in the 1950s and 1960s?

5. What are comets?

6. What will Prospector look for on the moon?

7. Who was the first human on the moon?

8. What did Americans bring back from the moon?

9. What is Clementine?

10. Do scientists think humans could live on the moon someday?

READING

Find out more about **scanning** by looking in the Reference Guide to Reading Strategies on pages xii–xiv.

Scanning

Scanning means looking for specific information in a reading. Scan the reading again, and complete the information in the following table.

1. The amount of rocks brought back from the moon by 1972 _____

2. The distance away from the moon that Prospector will fly _____

3. The length of time Prospector will spend orbiting the moon _____

4. The number of Americans who have walked on the moon _____

5. The number of astronauts on Prospector _____

6. The portion of the moon that has been mapped in detail _____

7. The weight of Prospector _____

8. The year Clementine was launched _____

9. The year of the first lunar landing _____

10. The year of the last U.S. mission to the moon _____

VOCABULARY
No Dictionaries!

Review the reading, looking for the words listed here. Look at the context in which each word is used. Write a definition next to it. Don't look up the words! Try to write your definitions in your own words.

1. *astronomer* _____

_____

2. *comets* _____

_____

3. *crater* _____

_____

4. *glimpses* _____

_____

5. *magnetism* _____

_____

6. *penguins* _____

_____

7. *telescopes* _____

_____

THINK ABOUT IT

1. Why do you think people are fascinated by the moon?

2. Would you live on the moon if you could?

3. Why do you think it's important to find out more about the moon? (Or do you think it's not important?)

PART TWO

Life Online

The Internet is changing the way people live. It is opening up
new worlds of information and communication.
This section looks at some of the influence of the Internet.

Before You Read

Estimated Number of Internet Users, by Country

Mexico	29,000
Philippines	100,000
Thailand	120,000
Slovenia	142,000
Portugal	200,000
People's Republic of China	300,000
Norway	500,000
Singapore	500,000
New Zealand	560,000
Malaysia	600,000
Russia	600,000
South Africa	600,000
Italy	700,000
Poland	700,000
South Korea	730,000
Spain	802,000
Brazil	1,000,000
Australia	1,210,000
Taiwan	1,260,000
Netherlands	1,300,000
France	1,400,000
Sweden	1,900,000
Germany	5,800,000
Canada	8,000,000
United Kingdom	10,000,000
Japan	12,100,000
United States	62,000,000

Source: ITM Solutions, Inc.
(http://www.lsilink.com)

Look at the table and answer these questions:

1. What country surprises you most?

2. Is your country listed? Do you think the number of Internet users in your country is growing?

3. How quickly do you think Internet use is growing?

In the following article, taken from a book called *Netiquette*, the author discusses some of the problems with e-mail communication. Before you read this passage, think about the following questions:

- Do you use a computer regularly? What do you use it for?
- Do you think it is important to understand how to use computers?
- Do we lose something when we communicate by using computers?

Cultural Cues

Netiquette = Inter**net** + e**tiquette**. Proper Internet behavior.

Cyberspace = The imaginary "space" created by computers that are connected to each other; in cyberspace, you can write e-mail, see web pages, do research, and many other things.

The golden rule "Treat other people the way you want them to treat you."

The Rules of Netiquette
by Virginia Shea

So, you got a **modem**[1] for your birthday and you want to make some new **on-line**[2] friends. Where do you start?

Rule 1: Remember the human

The golden rule your parents and teachers taught you was pretty simple:
5 *Do unto others as you'd have others do unto you.* Imagine how you would feel if you were in the other person's shoes. Stand up for yourself, but try not to hurt people's feelings.

In **cyberspace,** we state this in an even more basic manner:
Remember the human.
10 When you communicate by using a computer, all you see is a computer screen. You can't use facial expressions, gestures, or tone of voice to communicate your meaning. Words are all you have. The same is true for the person who is writing to you.

When you are talking on-line—whether it's an e-mail message or a re-
15 sponse to a discussion group—it is easy to misinterpret meaning. It's too easy to forget that your **correspondent**[3] is a person with feelings like your own.

Computers bring people together who might never meet in real life. But the way of communicating makes the exchange less personal. Humans
20 writing e-mail often behave the way some people behave when they drive a car: They curse at other drivers, make obscene gestures, and behave badly. Most of them would never act that way at work or at home. But the computer (or the car) seems to make it okay.

The message of netiquette is that it is not acceptable. Yes, use your
25 computer to express yourself freely, explore new worlds, and boldly go where you've never gone before. But remember the main rule of Netiquette: Those are real people out there.

Would you say it to the person's face?

Writer Guy Kawasaki tells a story about getting e-mail from a man he has
30 never met. On-line, the man tells Guy that he's a bad writer who has nothing interesting to say.

Rude? Yes, but unfortunately, this happens all the time in cyberspace.

---

[1]modem = device that connects computers together by phone lines

[2]on-line = connected to the Internet

[3]correspondent = a person who writes a letter or message

Maybe it's the power of sending mail to a well-known writer like Kawasaki. Maybe it's the fact that you can't see his disappointed face as he reads
35 your cruel words. Whatever the reason, it's too common.

Guy proposes a useful test for anything you are about to write on-line:
Ask yourself, "Would I say this to the person's face?" If the answer is no,
rewrite it and reread it. Repeat the process. When you are sure that you
would say these words to the person directly, then you can send it through
40 cyberspace.

**Check Your
Comprehension**

1. What is the "golden rule" and how does it apply to proper behavior on
   the Internet?

2. What is cyberspace?

3. Who is Guy Kawasaki?

4. In what ways do some people behave badly on the Internet?

5. What "test" does Kawasaki propose?

 **READING**

Find out more about
summarizing by
looking in the
Reference Guide to
Reading Strategies on
pages xii–xiv.

Summarizing

Summarizing can help you to understand the main ideas of a reading. In
the following space write a summary of this article. Don't use any more
space than this.

_____

_____

_____

_____

_____

Compare your summary to a classmate's. How are they different? Do you
want to change your summary in any way?

VOCABULARY
Crossword Puzzle

The following crossword puzzle uses words from the reading. Can you find the answers? Work with a partner if that helps. Read the clues, then put one letter in each blank. Consult the reading again if you need to.

NETIQUETTE

Across

2. Devices that connect computers to telephone lines

8. Facial _____; looks that show a mood or feeling

9. Not polite

10. To go _____; connected to the Internet

Down

1. The place where computers meet

3. A talk, either on-line or between people

4. Emotions or sentiments

5. A keyboard + a monitor + memory

6. Meaningful movement

7. The _____ rule: "Do unto others . . ."

11. Messages sent by computer

THINK ABOUT IT

1. Why do you think people might be more rude on-line than when talking face-to-face?

2. How has e-mail changed the way people communicate, in your opinion?

3. Look at the following e-mail message. Do you think this writer "remembered the human"? If not, rewrite the message so that it is more polite.

Date: September 12

To: Jacob Gillette

From: Margo Lincoln

Subject: Your Report

Dear Jacob,

I got the report you finished last week. It is so sloppy! Can't you do better work? I can't believe you took all week to write something so unprofessional. I hope you will rewrite it right away!

Before You Read

On-Line Use

Percentage of Americans who use Internet services:	20.0%
Percentage of Americans who have used the Internet in the past 30 days:	13.9%
Percentage of women who have been on-line in the past 30 days:	12.5%
Percentage of men who have been on-line in the past 30 days:	15.5%
Percentage who spent more than 20 hours on-line:	18.4%
Percentage who spent 10-19 hours on-line:	15.2%
Percentage who spent 5-9 hours on-line:	24.4%
Percentage who spent less than 5 hours on-line:	42.4%

Source: *E&P Interactive*

In the next reading, the author examines a new problem: people who are "addicted" to the Internet.

Before you read, think about the following questions:

- Consult the chart. Do you think that "Internet addiction" is a big problem?

- Do you know someone who uses the Internet a lot?

- How much Internet use is too much?

Cultural Cues

British Columbia The province of Canada that is on the Pacific Ocean north of Washington State.

support group A group of people who share a common problem and meet to discuss how to solve their problems

by Pam Belluck Net Addicti⊙n?

Not long ago, in a drug and alcohol **rehabilitation**[1] center in Texas, a 17-year-old boy was going through withdrawal. His body **shuddered**[2] with **convulsions**[3]. He threw tables and chairs around the hospital. Was he hooked on heroin? Cocaine? Whiskey? Cigarettes?

5   No, his psychologist said. The teen-ager was **withdrawing**[4] from the Internet.

A woman's husband divorced her because she spent too much time on the Internet . But, she continued to surf the World Wide Web. She did this so often that she forgot to take her children to the doctor or get the kids

10   enough food. Her husband asked the court for the children.

But he needed someone to support her illness. "I had to write a letter to the judge," said Dr. Jonathan Kandell, a psychologist. "The judge did not believe there was such a thing as Internet addiction."

Is there? Some psychologists say that Internet addiction is real—just

15   like gambling or drug abuse.

At the University of Maryland, a doctor started an Internet addiction **support group** after he watched a few addicted students nearly fail school.

How can you tell if you have an **abnormal**[5] pattern of Internet use? Do you need to spend increased amounts of time on the Internet to achieve

---

[1]rehabilitation = recovery from illness

[2]shuddered = shook

[3]convulsions = sudden, violent uncontrollable body movement

[4]withdrawing = removing oneself from

[5]abnormal = not normal, unusual

20 satisfaction? And when you're not on-line, do you have fantasies or dreams about the Internet?

Tyler Johnson, 17, a high school senior in Abbotsford, **British Columbia,** spends more than six hours a day on-line and more than an hour reading his e-mail.

25 Tyler dropped out of school sports, and now, every day after school until 3 or 4 o'clock in the morning, he plays games on the Internet.

Dr. Kandell **speculates**[6] that many addicts don't get help because they don't know they have a problem. "I think we're about a year away from having people recognize it's really a problem," he said. "It's out there. There's 30 no question."

Source: *The New York Times*

Check Your Comprehension

1. Who is Dr. Kandell?

2. What was the Texas boy's illness?

3. What does Dr. Kandell believe?

4. Why did Dr. Kandell write a letter to the judge?

5. What are some of the symptoms of Internet addiction, according to the article?

 READING

Find out more about **find the main idea** by looking in the Reference Guide to Reading Strategies on pages xii–xiv.

Finding the Main Idea

What do you think the main idea of this story is? Is there more than one? Write a paragraph about the main ideas of this story.

_____

_____

_____

_____

_____

_____

_____

_____

Review your paragraph. Compare your answers with a partner's.

[6]speculates = guesses

VOCABULARY
Understanding Idioms and Colloquial Language

You will find the following words and phrases in the reading. Use each of these words or phrases in a sentence. Be sure that your sentence shows that you understand the meaning.

1. *drop out*
2. *hooked on*
3. *surf (the web)*
4. *withdrawal*

1. _____
2. _____
3. _____
4. _____

THINK ABOUT IT

1. Do you think Internet addiction is real?

2. What is something you enjoy a lot? (Candy? Sports? Movies?) Are you "addicted" to it? Explain your answer.

3. Take a poll. Talk to three men and three women at your school or in your family who use the Internet. Ask them the following questions:

   1. Do you spend a lot of time on the Internet?

   2. When you're not on-line, do you have fantasies or dreams about the Internet?

   3. How many hours a day do you use the Internet?

   4. Do you think you neglect your family or job because of the Internet?

When you complete your surveys, combine your answers with the answers your classmates got. What patterns do you see?

Answer these questions:

1. Who used the Internet more, men or women?

2. Did anyone show symptoms of Internet addiction?

Write a report on your findings.

S Y N T H E S I S

Discussion and Debate

1. What is your attitude toward technology: do new technologies interest you? Why or why not?

2. Do you enjoy science fiction? If so, what science fiction movies, books, or television shows do you enjoy?

3. Do you prefer to do things the most modern way, or using more old-fashioned methods? For example, do you prefer writing letters to sending e-mail? Do you microwave your dinner, or use an oven? Why?

Writing Topics

1. Think about one type of technology, such as a personal computer or a cellular phone, that you depend on. In your journal, describe what your day would be like without it.

2. What do you imagine a day in space might be like? Write a page or two describing what you think it might be like to live in space.

3. How has technology changed your life recently? Write an essay in which you describe what changes in technology have made an important difference recently.

On Your Own

1. Interview five people. Ask them these questions, and any of your own you want to add.
   - Do you use the Internet?
   - Do you think space travel is worth the expense?
   - Would you live in space if you had the opportunity?

   Compare your answers to your classmates' answers.

2. Many movies have been made about space exploration or alien life. Check out one of these videos from a library or video store and watch it. Discuss it with your class.

2001: A Space Odyssey	*Contact*
The Right Stuff	*Close Encounters of the Third Kind*
Apollo 13	*Star Trek*

3. On the Internet, you can find out more about space. Look at http://www.nasa.gov to see new information about the space program. If you don't have access to the Internet, look in your library.

4. Interview an older person. Ask him or her about the five most important technological changes in his or her lifetime. How would you answer the same question?

★★

A L M A N A C For additional cultural information, refer to the Almanac on pages 207–222. The Almanac contains lists of useful facts, maps, and other information to enhance your learning.

CHAPTER 10

Popular Culture

American popular culture is made up of many forms of entertainment including: television, sports, cartoons, movies, fashion, and more. In this chapter, you'll read about television and movies, two important parts of American popular culture.

PART ONE

Television: You Are What You Watch

Television is one of the strongest influences in American culture. People discuss programs at work and with friends, and many people feel like they "know" the television characters in their favorite shows. American television enjoys popularity all over the world.

Before You Read

Television-Owning Countries in the World

Country	Homes with Television
China	227,500,000
United States	94,200,000
Russia	48,269,000
Japan	41,328,000
Brazil	38,880,000
Germany	36,295,000
India	35,000,000
Great Britain	22,446,000
France	21,667,000
Italy	20,812,000

Source: Nielsen Media Research

Do you watch a lot of television? Have you ever gone for a week without it? The next reading talks about what it's like to go without television for a week. *Note:* The television programs mentioned in this story are not real.

Before you read, think about these questions:
- How much television do you watch every week?
- Do you think children watch too much television?

Cultural Cues

Monopoly A popular board game in which players buy and sell property until someone owns all the property. The property is patterned after Atlantic City, New Jersey.

Boardwalk and Park Place The names of "properties" you can buy in the game of Monopoly

Unplugged

by Harriet Diller

Mom gave me the bad news on Monday morning.

"No television this week, Teddy," she said with a smile. "We're taking part in the library's Great TV Turn-Off."

"We're what?" I asked.

5   "It's an experiment," Mom said. "To see what families do when there's no TV to watch. We're all supposed to keep a diary of what it's like to go without TV for a week."

I frowned. "Couldn't we do some other kind of experiment? I'd rather find out how long I can stand having my teeth drilled at the dentist's. If I 10 can watch TV while they're doing the drilling."

"Sorry, Ted," Mom said. "The librarians are very interested in the results of this project."

Remind me never to go to that library again," I said as Mom started writing something on a big piece of paper. "What's that?"

15   "A poster," Mom said. "Would you mind taping it over the TV screen?"

I minded a lot, but I did what Mom said. The sign said **DO NOT WATCH THIS TV IF YOU VALUE YOUR LIFE.**

I valued my life plenty, so I didn't touch the TV when I came home from school that day. I didn't dare. The Great TV Turn-Off had taken over the 20 whole town. No one was watching. Thanks to the library.

"My diary is going to be some interesting reading," I told Mom as I helped her peel potatoes for supper. "Got up. Went to school. Came home. Died of **terminal**[1] boredom."

Mom laughed. "You're not dying of terminal boredom. You're helping me 25 fix supper. I, for one, like it. When was the last time you helped me fix supper instead of watching television?"

I had to admit I couldn't remember. That night I went up to bed early and opened the diary Mom had given me to write in. What else was there to do? So I wrote.

30   Monday. Helped Mom with supper. Had supper in the kitchen instead of on TV tray while watching *The Incredible Clod*[2]. Helped Mom with dishes. Did homework. Somebody help me. Please! There's nothing fun to do around this place.

There wasn't a whole lot to write in my diary the next day either, but I 35 wrote in it anyway.

---

[1]terminal = deadly, fatal

[2]clod = clumsy or stupid person

Tuesday. Got tired of staring at **DO NOT WATCH TV** sign. Went outside. Found some old boards and built a fort with Dan and Ray. After supper, I cleaned my room without being asked. I must be going mad.

By Wednesday, I was in the habit of writing in my diary.

40   Wednesday. Blew the dust off some old games on the shelf. Invited Dan and Ray to come over and play **Monopoly.** Played for two hours. Your faithful diary writer is now the owner of **Boardwalk and Park Place.**

Thursday. Mom said I could make **fudge**[3] as long as I didn't turn on the stove. She said I'm a fire hazard. Found a recipe for no-cook fudge.

45   Even Mom and Dad agreed it was good.

Friday. Broke down and walked downtown to that place—the library. Checked out two mysteries. Finished off the fudge while I read mysteries.

Saturday. You are reading the diary of a desperate man. Tell me what there is to do on a Saturday morning besides watch cartoons.

50   Later on Saturday. Finally found something to do. Cleaned out my closet. Mom said it was all right to set up a yard sale outside. I sold almost all the stuff I cleaned out of my closet.

Sunday. Took big bucks earned from yard sale downtown. Bought two model airplanes and two mysteries. Dad helped me put together one of the

55   airplanes. Later I helped Mom bake a chocolate cake. I ate cake and drank milk while reading mysteries. Talk about heaven.

Monday. Your faithful diary writer is in **a state of shock**[4]. Mom just reminded me that today is the end of the Great TV Turn-Off. Please, faithful reader, don't think I'm weird. But I don't think I'll turn on the TV today. I've

60   got this mystery I want to finish reading. And another model airplane to put together.

Maybe the Great TV Turn-Off has pickled my brain. I don't even care if I miss my favorite movie of all time, *The Invasion of the Giant Cucumbers*. It's supposed to be on TV tonight. But I've already seen it seven times. I might

65   watch TV tomorrow. Or I might not. I might find something better to do.

Source: Highlights for Children, Inc.

Check Your Comprehension

1. What is the meaning of "unplugged"?

2. Why did the town stop watching television?

3. How does Ted feel about the experiment?

4. What does the narrator mean by "died of terminal boredom"?

5. How did the narrator change by the end of the story?

[3]fudge = a type of chocolate candy

[4]in a state of shock = surprised

READING

Find out more about **summarizing** by looking in the Reference Guide to Reading Strategies on pages xii–xiv.

Summarizing

Reread the article. **Summarize** the events of Teddy's life without television. The first one is done for you.

Life Without TV

1. _Teddy helped his mother make dinner._ _____

2. _____

3. _____

4. _____

5. _____

7. _____

8. _____

9. _____

10. _____

VOCABULARY
Confusing Pairs

The following pairs of words or phrases can sometimes be confusing. Choose the correct word or phrase to complete the sentence.

1. *reminded* and *remembered*

   He _____ to do the dishes.

   He _____ his brother to do his homework.

2. *breaks down* and *breaks*

   A glass plate _____ easily.

   My car often _____ on the highway.

3. *check out* and *check in*

   He asked me to _____ with him later.

   I like to _____ books from the library.

4. *go mad* and *get mad*

   If I can't watch television, I think I'll _____ from boredom.

   If my room isn't clean, my mother will _____ .

THINK ABOUT IT

1. Why is "Unplugged!" a good title for this story?

2. If you went for a week without television, what would you do instead?

3. Do you think children watch too much television? Explain your answer.

Before You Read

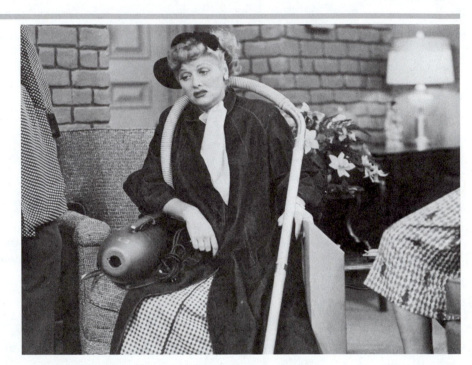

Watch the CNN video on Lucille Ball.

Discuss these questions.

1. Why is Lucille Ball so popular?

2. What event does this newscast report on?

3. Who is Lucie Arnaz?

The following reading has two parts: the words to the "I Love Lucy" theme song, and a brief outline of Lucille Ball's life.

Before you read, think about the following questions:

- Have you seen the "I Love Lucy" show?
- Do you enjoy old television comedies?

I Love Lucy

The Theme Song from the *I Love Lucy* Show

I love Lucy and she loves me
We're as happy as two can be
Sometimes we quarrel but then
5   How we love making up again

Lucy kisses like no one can
She's my Mrs. and I'm her man
And life is heaven you see
'cause I love Lucy
10   Yes I love Lucy
and Lucy loves me

Lucille Ball

Lucille Ball was born in 1910, in Celaron, New York. She left school at age 15 to become an actress. However, her early career was unsuccessful, so
15   she turned to modeling. She used the name Diane Belmont. Her modeling career led to her first movie role, in *Roman Scandals* (1934). She appeared in many movies and radio programs after that. However, she didn't become really successful until 1951. That was the year that she teamed up with her Cuban husband, Desi Arnaz, to play the funny middle-class couple, Lucy
20   and Ricky Ricardo.

    I Love Lucy was a classic television situation comedy. The redheaded Lucy was considered a comic genius when she played the **ditzy**[1] housewife Lucy. The show lasted for 179 episodes. A 1953 episode was about the birth of their TV son, "Little Ricky." This show was filmed to **coincide**[2] with the
25   birth of her real-life son, Desi Arnaz, Jr. This episode attracted more viewers than the **inauguration**[3] of President Dwight D. Eisenhower, which was on at the same time.

    Lucy and her husband founded Desilu Productions in 1950. Lucy became a successful independent producer of television shows. Many people find

[1]ditzy = silly
[2]coincide = happen at the same time
[3]inauguration = swearing in

30 it surprising that the woman who played the **nutty**[4] housewife was one of
the most successful businesswomen in Hollywood.

She divorced Arnaz in 1960, and then appeared on Broadway in the play
Wildcat. But, she quickly returned to television, and starred in two other
successful **sitcoms**[5], *The Lucy Show* (1962–68) and *Here's Lucy* (1968–73).

35 She continued to appear on television specials until her death in 1989.

Check Your Comprehension

1. How did Lucille Ball start her career?

2. When did Lucille Ball begin to be very successful?

3. What types of characters did Lucille Ball often play?

4. What fact about Lucille Ball surprises many people?

5. How many television sitcoms did Lucille Ball star in?

 **READING**

Find out more about **understanding processes** by looking in the Reference Guide to Reading Strategies on pages xii–xiv.

Understanding Processes

Review the reading and complete the following time line to help you remember and **understand the process.** The first event is written for you.

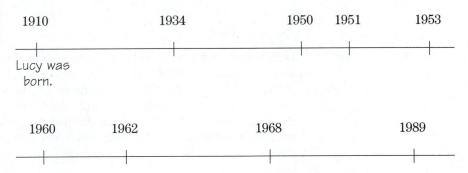

1910   1934   1950   1951   1953

Lucy was born.

1960   1962   1968   1989

[4]nutty = silly, crazy

[5]sitcom = situation comedy, usually a half-hour show

VOCABULARY
No Dictionaries!

Locate the following words in the reading. Without using your dictionary, write a short definition of each. Look at the way the word is used in the sentence to determine what the word means. Include an example sentence, showing you understand the meaning.

1. *episode* _____

   Example sentence: _____

2. *inauguration* _____

   Example sentence: _____

3. *sitcom* _____

   Example sentence: _____

4. *coincide* _____

   Example sentence: _____

5. *ditzy* _____

   Example sentence: _____

6. *quarrel* _____

   Example sentence: _____

THINK ABOUT IT

1. Do you enjoy older, "classic" comedies more than modern ones? Why or why not?

2. *I Love Lucy* still appears on television in most cities. Check your television listings to see when it is on. If you can, watch an episode. Discuss this with the class.

3. When *I Love Lucy* was first on television, many television executives were worried about its content. She was the first woman on television who talked about being pregnant (though they never used the word *pregnant.*) How has television changed since then? Think of examples of modern shows.

PART TWO

MOVIES: The Silver Screen

Movies, are one of the United States' biggest exports
to the rest of the world. Many American movies
are considered "classics" and are well-known
internationally.

Before You Read

To Kill a Mockingbird

In this reading, you will read part of the script from *To Kill A Mocking-bird*. This story was written by Harper Lee in the early 1960s. Horton Foote helped turn it into one of the most popular and important films of all times.

Before you read, think about these questions:
- Have you seen or read *To Kill a Mockingbird*?
- What is your favorite film?

About the Author

Horton Foote was born in Wharton, Texas in 1916. He moved to New York and studied acting, but quickly discovered writing. He was awarded two Academy Awards for his writing of *To Kill a Mockingbird* (1962) and *Tender Mercies* (1983).

READING

Find out more about **reading aloud** by looking in the Reference Guide to Reading Strategies on pages xii–xiv.

Reading Aloud

Reading aloud can help you hear the words better, and it can help you understand a reading more fully. This reading is a script, that is, a dialogue spoken by characters in a movie. Practice reading it aloud. You can do this by yourself, or with others taking different parts. The parts in *italics* describe the scene.

Cultural Cues

the crash The stock market crash of 1929; it was the beginning of the Great Depression, a time of great poverty in the United States.

Methodist A type of Christian religion.

tire swing A swing made by hanging an old tire by a rope to a tree.

nothing to fear but fear itself A reference to a speech by President Franklin D. Roosevelt in which he tried to calm people's fears about the Depression.

TO KILL A MOCKINGBIRD

Screenplay adaption by Horton Foote

It is just before dawn, and in the half-light cotton farms, pinewoods, the hills surrounding Maycomb, and the Courthouse Square are seen. A young woman's voice is heard.

5

Jean Louise: Maycomb was a tired old town, even in 1932 . . . when I first knew it. Somehow it was hotter then. Men's stiff collars wilted[1] by nine in the morning. Ladies bathed before noon and after their three o'clock naps. And by nightfall they were like soft teacakes with frosting

---

[1]wilted = sagged, collapsed in the heat

from sweating and sweet **talcum**[2]. The day was twenty-four hours long, but it seemed longer. There's no hurry, for there's nowhere to go and

10   nothing to buy . . . and no money to buy it with. Although Maycomb County had recently been told that it had **nothing to fear but fear itself.**

*(The Finch house and yard are seen. It is a small **frame house**[3], built high off the ground and with a porch in the manner of Southern cottages of its day. The yard is a large one, filled with oaks, and it has an air of*

15   *mystery about it in the early morning light.)*

That summer, I was six years old.

(WALTER CUNNINGHAM, *a thin, **raw-boned**[4] farmer in his late fifties, comes into view. He is carrying a **crokersack**[5] full of hickory nuts. He passes under the oak tree at the side of the house.* SCOUT, *six, dressed in*

20   *blue jeans, drops from one of its branches to the ground. She brushes herself off and goes toward* MR. CUNNINGHAM.)

Scout: Good Morning, Mr. Cunningham.

Cunningham: Mornin' Miss.

Scout: My daddy is getting dressed. Would you like me to call him for you?

25 *Cunningham:* No, Miss . . . I . . . don't care to bother.

Scout: Why, it's no bother, Mr. Cunningham. He'll be happy to see you. Atticus. (SCOUT *hurries up the steps and opens the door.*) Atticus, here's Mr. Cunningham.

(SCOUT *steps back onto the porch as* ATTICUS *enters.* WALTER CUNNINGHAM

30   *seems ill at ease and embarrassed.*)

Atticus: Good morning, Walter.

Cunningham: Good morning, Mr. Finch. I . . . didn't want to bother you none. I **brung**[6] you these hickory nuts as part of my **entailment**[7].

Atticus (*reaching for the sack of nuts*): Well, I thank you. The **collards**[8]

35   we had last week were delicious.

Cunningham (*gesturing, and then turning to leave*): Well, good morning.

Atticus: Good morning, Walter.

(Atticus *holds the sack of nuts.* SCOUT *is on the steps behind him.* SCOUT *leans on* ATTICUS' *shoulders as they watch* MR. CUNNINGHAM *leave.*)

---

[2]talcum = powder

[3]frame house = wooden house

[4]raw-boned = thin, with bones showing

[5]crokersack = a type of cloth sack for carrying food

[6]brung = brought, this is an ungrammatical form

[7]entailment = bill

[8]collards = a type of green vegetable

40   Scout, I think maybe next time Mr. Cunningham comes, you better not call me.

Scout: Well, I thought you'd want to thank him.

Atticus: Oh, I do. I think it embarrasses him to be thanked.

(ATTICUS *turns and puts the sack on the porch and starts for the front yard* 45 *to get the morning papers.* SCOUT *follows after him.*)

Scout: Why does he bring you all this stuff?

Atticus: He is paying me for some legal work I did for him.

Scout: Why is he paying you like this?

Atticus: That's the only way he can . . . he has no money.

50   (ATTICUS *comes back to the porch as* SCOUT *follows. He picks up the newspaper and reads.*)

Scout: Is he poor?

Atticus: Yes.

Scout: Are we poor?

55   *Atticus:* We are indeed.

Scout: Are we as poor as the Cunninghams?

Atticus: No, not exactly. The Cunninghams are country folks, farmers, and **the crash** hit them the hardest.

(CALPURNIA, *in her late fifties, appears at the screen door.*)

60   *Calpurnia:* Scout, call your brother. (*She goes back inside.*)

Scout: Atticus, Jem is up in the tree. He says he won't come down until you agree to play football for the **Methodists.**

(ATTICUS *walks toward the tree. In a treehouse, high up in the tree, sits* JEM. *He is ten, with a serious, manly little face. Right now, he is* **scowling**⁹.)

65   *Atticus:* Jem . . . Son, why don't you come on down and have your breakfast? Calpurnia has a good one . . . hot biscuits.

Jem: No Sir. Not until you agree to play football for the Methodists.

(ATTICUS *is looking up at* JEM. SCOUT *is swinging in the* **tire swing**.)

Atticus: Oh, no, Son. I can't do that. I explained to you I'm too old to get 70   out there. After all, I'm the only father you have. You wouldn't want me to get out there and get my head knocked off, would you?

Jem: I ain't coming down.

Atticus: Suit yourself.

---

⁹scowling = frowning

Check Your Comprehension

1. Who is Scout?

2. Who is Atticus?

3. Who is Jem?

4. What kind of work does Atticus Finch do?

5. Why did Mr. Cunningham visit the Finches?

6. What is Mr. Cunningham like?

7. Why doesn't Atticus want Scout to call him when Mr. Cunningham comes over?

8. Why is Jem in a tree?

9. Why won't Atticus play football?

VOCABULARY Using New Words

The following words can be found in the reading. Review the reading and be sure you know what they mean. Then, complete the sentences, showing you know what the words mean.

1. If you get up at **dawn,** it's probably _____ o'clock.

2. There are _____ **surrounding** my house.

3. You use **talcum** after _____ .

4. A **cottage** is a _____ .

5. I saw him **scowl** when _____ .

6. **Biscuits** are _____ .

7. My father said, "**Suit yourself,**" when _____

_____ .

THINK ABOUT IT

1. Have you ever owed someone money and not been able to pay it back right away? If so, how did you feel?

2. Would you rather owe money to someone or have someone owe money to you? Why?

3. Jem says he is staying up in the tree until his father does what he wants him to do. Why do children do things like that?

Before You Read

The Wicked Witch and Dorothy in Oz

The Wizard of Oz: Plot Summary

Dorothy lives on a farm in Kansas with her stern Auntie Em. (In the film, her life on the farm is filmed in black and white.) A tornado arrives, and picks her and her dog up and deposits them in the land of Oz. Things in Oz are strange and beautiful (the film now turns to color). She meets strange characters like the Cowardly Lion, the Tin Man, and the Scarecrow. But Dorothy just wants to get back home. She finally discovers she has the power to go back home on her own by clicking her red shoes together. When she gets back to Kansas, the film becomes black and white again.

In this reading, Terry McMillan, the author of *Waiting to Exhale*, talks about a movie that was very important to her.

Before you read this essay, think about these questions:
- How important are movies to you?
- What is your favorite movie? Why?

About the Author

Terry McMillan was born in 1951 in Michigan. She attended the University of California, Berkeley from 1973 to 1979. Then she moved to New York to study film at Columbia University, where she earned a Master's degree. In 1988, she became a professor at the University of Arizona. Her first book, *Mama*, was published in 1987. Her second book was *Disappearing Acts* (1989). McMillan's third novel, *Waiting to Exhale* (1992), has sold nearly four million copies and was made into a movie in 1995. McMillan's next book, *How Stella Got Her Groove Back*, (1996) was also made into a movie.

Cultural Cues

the thumb of Michigan   The state of Michigan looks like a hand, so part of the state has the shape of a thumb

READING

Find out more about **skimming** by looking in the Reference Guide to Reading Strategies on pages xii–xiv.

Skimming

Skimming means reading quickly to get the main ideas. Skim this article— take no more than four minutes to read it. Remember, keep your eyes moving, and read words in groups. Then answer these questions:

- What kind of home did McMillan grow up in?
- What was McMillan's family like?
- Why did she like *The Wizard of Oz?*

After answering these questions, return to the reading and read more carefully.

by Terry McMillan The Movie That Changed My Life:
The Wizard of Oz

I grew up in a small **industrial**[1] town in the **thumb of Michigan:** Port Huron. We had barely gotten used to the idea of color TV. I can guess how old I was when I first saw *The*
5 *Wizard of Oz* on TV because I remember the

house we lived in when I was still in elementary school. It was a huge, drafty house that had a fireplace we never once lit. We lived on two acres of land, and at the edge of the backyard
10 was the woods, which I always thought of as a forest. We had weeping willow trees, plum and pear trees, and blackberry bushes. We could not see into our neighbors' homes. Rail-

[1]industrial = with manufacturing companies

road tracks were part of our front yard, and
15 the house shook when a train passed—twice,
sometimes three times a day. You couldn't hear
the TV at all when it zoomed by, and I was
often afraid that if it ever flew off the tracks,
it would land on the sun porch, where we all
20 watched TV. I often left the room during this
time, but my younger sisters and brother
thought I was just scared. I think I was in the
third grade around this time.

It was a **raggedy**[2] house which really
25 should've been condemned, but we fixed it up
and kept it clean. We had our **German Shepherd**[3], Prince, who slept under the **rickety**[4]
steps to the side porch that were **on the verge
of**[5] collapsing but never did. I remember performing a ritual whenever Oz was coming on.
30 I either baked cookies or cinnamon rolls or
popped popcorn while all five of us waited for
Dorothy to spin from black and white on that
dreary[6] farm in Kansas to the **luminous**[7] land
35 of color of Oz.

My house was chaotic, especially with four
sisters and brothers and a mother who worked
at a factory, and if I'm remembering correctly,
my father was there for the first few years of
40 the Oz (until he got **tuberculosis**[8] and had to
live in a **sanitarium**[9] for a year). I do recall
the noise and the fighting of my parents (not
to mention my other relatives and neighbors).
Violence was plentiful, and I wanted to go
45 wherever Dorothy was going where she would
not find trouble. To put it bluntly, I wanted to
escape because I needed an escape.

The initial thing I remember striking me
about Oz was how nasty Dorothy's Auntie Em

50 talked to her and everybody on the farm. I
was used to that **authoritative**[10] tone of voice
because my mother talked to us the same way.
She never asked you to do anything; she gave
you a command and never said "please," and,
55 once you finished it, rarely said "thank you."
The tone of her voice was always **hostile**[11],
and Auntie Em sounded just like my mother—
bossy and domineering. What little freedom we
had was snatched away. As a child, I often felt
60 helpless, powerless, because I had no control
over my situation and couldn't tell my mother
when I thought (or knew) she was wrong or
being totally unfair, or when her behavior was
inappropriate. I hated this feeling to no end,
65 but what was worse was not being able to do
anything about it except keep my mouth shut.

So I completely identified when no one had
time to listen to Dorothy. That dog's safety was
important to her, but no one seemed to think
70 that what Dorothy was saying could possibly
be as urgent as the situation at hand. When I
was younger, I rarely had the opportunity to
finish a sentence before my mother would cut
me off or complete it for me, or worse, give
75 me something to do. So when Dorothy's Auntie
Em dismisses her and tells her to find somewhere where she'll stay out of trouble, and
little Dorothy starts thinking about if there in
fact is such a place—one that is trouble free—I
80 was right there with her, because I wanted to
know, too.

I was afraid for Dorothy when she decided
to run away, but at the same time I was glad.
I couldn't much blame her—I mean, what kind
85 of life did she have, from what I'd seen so far?
She lived on an ugly farm out in the middle
of nowhere with all these old people who did
nothing but **chores**[12], chores, and more chores.
Who did she have to play with besides that
90 dog? And even though I lived in a house full

---

[2]raggedy = old, in poor condition

[3]German Shepherd = a type of large dog

[4]rickety = not sturdy, wobbly

[5]on the verge of = nearly

[6]dreary = boring, dull

[7]luminous = light filled, colorful

[8]tuberculosis = a serious disease of the lungs

[9]sanitarium = a place for people with contagious diseases
to recover

[10]authoritative = strong, commanding

[11]hostile = angry

[12]chores = jobs, tasks

of people, I knew how lonely Dorothy felt, or at least how isolated she must have felt. First of all, I was the oldest, and my sisters and brother were ignorant and silly creatures who 95 often bored me because they couldn't hold a decent conversation. I couldn't ask them questions, like: Why are we living in this dump? When is Mama going to get some more money? Why can't we go on vacations like other peo- 100 ple? Like white people? Why does our car always break down? Why are we poor? Why doesn't Mama ever laugh? Why do we have to live in Port Huron? Isn't there someplace better than this we can go live?

105   When Dorothy's house began to spin and spin and spin, I was curious as to where it was going to land. And to be honest, I didn't know little Dorothy was actually dreaming until she woke up and opened the door and everything 110 was in color! It looked like Paradise to me. The **foliage**[13] was almost an **iridescent**[14] green, the water bluer than I'd ever seen in any of the lakes in Michigan. Of course, once I realized she was in fact dreaming, it occurred to me 115 that this very well might be the only way to escape. To dream up another world. Create your own.

   At the time, I truly wished I could spin away from my family and home and land someplace 120 as beautiful and **surreal**[15] as Oz—if only for a little while. All I wanted was to get a chance to see another side of the world, to be able to make comparisons, and then decide if it was worth coming back home.

[13]foliage = leaves and grass

[14]iridescent = containing many colors

[15]surreal = fantastic, unbelievable

Check Your Comprehension

1. What was McMillan's home life like?

2. Where was McMillan's father?

3. What was her house like?

4. How did McMillan feel about her sisters and brother?

5. Why did McMillan need "an escape" from her life?

6. Why did McMillan sympathize with Dorothy in the movie?

7. Why were movies important to McMillan?

VOCABULARY
New Words

The following words are found in the reading. Review the reading to be sure you know what the words mean. Then, fill in the blanks with the correct words or phrases.

| sanitarium | chores | iridescent | dreary |
| raggedy | surreal | foliage | authoritative |

1. The policeman had an _____ voice.

2. The sunset was full of bright, _____ colors.

3. Having the President of the United States visit our town was a

   _____ experience.

4. I usually do a lot of _____ on Saturday mornings.

5. If you're ill, you may spend several weeks in a _____ .

6. In fall, the _____ is often red and orange, instead of green.

7. That old chair looks terrible! What a _____ piece of furniture it is.

8. The weather can be very _____ in the winter.

THINK ABOUT IT

1. Why do you think McMillan became a writer?

2. Have you seen *The Wizard of Oz?* If so, did you enjoy it? Why?

3. Is there a movie that has "changed your life"?

SYNTHESIS

Discussion and Debate

1. Why do you think people enjoy television and movies so much?

2. Which movie do you think of as a truly American movie? Why?

3. Think of another question to ask your classmates about the ideas in this chapter.

Writing Topics

1. What is the last movie you saw? Write a plot summary of it.

2. In your journal, write about your favorite television show. Who are the characters? Why do you like the show?

3. Is television a good or a bad influence on people? Write an essay defending your opinion. Give examples of your points.

On Your Own

1. If you haven't seen *To Kill a Mockingbird* or *The Wizard of Oz,* check one of them out of the library or a video store. Watch it and discuss it with your class.

2. Ask 10 people to name their favorite movie and favorite television show. Also ask their age. (Don't ask for a specific age—some people find this rude. Ask if they are in their twenties, thirties, forties, etc.)

   Compile a list with your classmates. How do the choices compare to your own favorite movies and television shows? Does age seem to have an effect on people's choices?

3. On the Internet or in the library, do some research on your favorite film. What information did you find that you didn't know before? Check the Internet Movie Database (http://www.imdb.com).

4. For one week, keep a diary of your television watching. Write down every show you watch, and for how long. Describe the kind of shows you watch (comedy, drama, news, and so on). Bring your diary to class after a week to compare to your classmates'. What did you notice about your television watching?

★★

A L M A N A C For additional cultural information, refer to the Almanac on pages 207–222. The Almanac contains lists of useful facts, maps, and other information to enhance your learning.

ALMANAC

★★

1. Map of the United States showing state capitals

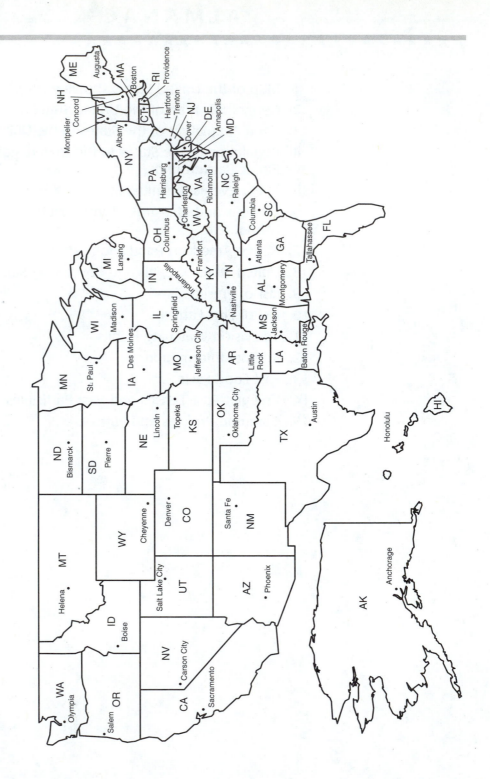

**2. Geographic map
of the United
States**

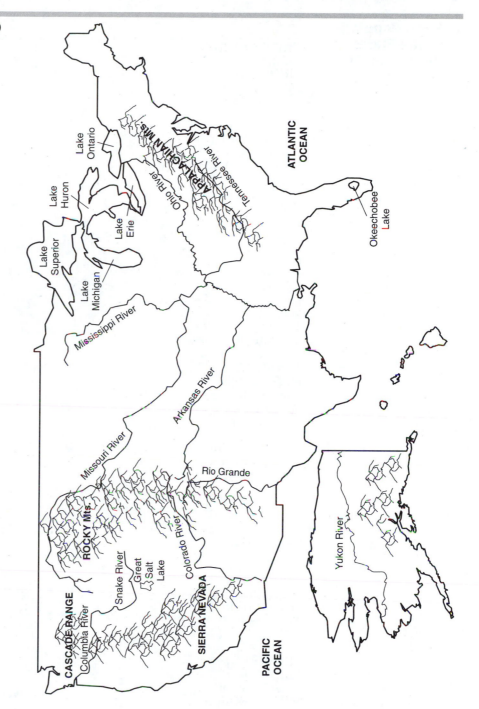

3. Total Population of the States in the United States

	Latest Estimate
UNITED STATES	248,709,873
ALABAMA	4,040,587
ARKANSAS	550,043
ARIZONA	3,665,228
ARKANSAS	2,350,725
CALIFORNIA	29,760,021
COLORADO	3,294,394
CONNECTICUT	3,287,116
DELAWARE	666,168
DISTRICT OF COLUMBIA	606,900
FLORIDA	12,937,926
GEORGIA	6,478,216
HAWAII	1,108,229
IDAHO	1,006,749
ILLINOIS	11,430,602
INDIANA	5,544,159
IOWA	2,776,755
KANSAS	2,477,574
KENTUCKY	3,685,296
LOUISIANA	4,219,973
MAINE	1,227,928
MARYLAND	4,781,468
MASSACHUSETTS	6,016,425
MICHIGAN	9,295,297
MINNESOTA	4,375,099
MISSISSIPPI	2,573,216
MISSOURI	5,117,073
MONTANA	799,065
NEBRASKA	1,578,385
NEVADA	1,201,833
NEW HAMPSHIRE	1,109,252
NEW JERSEY	7,730,188
NEW MEXICO	1,515,069
NEW YORK	17,990,455
NORTH CAROLINA	6,628,637
NORTH DAKOTA	638,800
OHIO	10,847,115
OKLAHOMA	3,145,585
OREGON	2,842,321
PENNSYLVANIA	11,881,643
RHODE ISLAND	1,003,464
SOUTH CAROLINA	3,486,703
SOUTH DAKOTA	696,004
TENNESSEE	4,877,185
TEXAS	16,986,510
UTAH	1,722,850
VERMONT	562,758
VIRGINIA	6,187,358
WASHINGTON	4,866,692
WEST VIRGINIA	1,793,477
WISCONSIN	4,891,769
WYOMING	453,588

Source: Population Estimates Branch, U.S. Bureau of the Census, Release date: Aug. 1996

4. Population of the States in the United States by Ethnic Background

	Total	Total Hispanic	White Total	White Hispanic	White non-Hispanic	Black	American Indian	Asian & Pacific Islander
UNITED STATES	265,283,783	28,268,895	219,748,786	25,771,113	199,977,673	33,503,435	2,288,119	9,743,443
ALABAMA	4,273,084	35,857	3,125,926	30,401	3,095,525	1,103,986	15,385	27,787
ALASKA	607,007	22,356	462,255	18,075	444,180	23,325	95,339	26,088
ARIZONA	4,428,068	941,479	3,936,621	880,294	3,056,327	153,888	248,490	89,069
ARKANSAS	2,509,793	40,852	2,076,142	36,088	2,040,054	403,466	13,170	17,015
CALIFORNIA	31,878,234	9,630,188	25,491,661	9,011,827	16,479,834	2,371,293	303,494	3,711,786
COLORADO	3,822,676	535,917	3,535,813	503,635	3,032,178	164,343	35,538	86,982
CONNECTICUT	3,274,238	253,245	2,895,483	223,705	2,671,778	297,984	7,906	72,865
DELAWARE	724,842	22,774	572,853	19,365	553,488	136,062	2,434	13,493
DISTRICT OF CO-LUMBIA	543,213	37,705	184,638	30,035	154,603	340,837	1,692	16,046
FLORIDA	14,399,985	2,022,110	11,930,830	1,879,468	10,051,362	2,172,252	51,592	245,311
GEORGIA	7,353,225	187,392	5,130,880	163,122	4,967,758	2,074,548	17,086	130,711
HAWAII	1,183,723	93,100	395,969	46,444	349,525	35,514	6,515	745,725
IDAHO	1,189,251	80,976	1,154,199	75,050	1,079,149	6,438	15,856	12,758
ILLINOIS	11,846,544	1,136,282	9,639,662	1,063,265	8,576,397	1,806,901	26,210	373,771
INDIANA	5,840,528	129,277	5,297,205	118,023	5,179,182	477,928	14,022	51,373
IOWA	2,851,792	49,865	2,754,355	45,164	2,709,191	55,047	8,358	34,032
KANSAS	2,572,150	124,842	2,355,375	112,989	2,242,386	152,166	22,903	41,706
KENTUCKY	3,883,723	28,543	3,573,069	24,406	3,548,663	279,930	5,891	24,833
LOUISIANA	4,350,579	109,969	2,884,225	94,301	2,789,924	1,393,678	19,346	53,330
MAINE	1,243,316	8,446	1,223,690	7,598	1,216,092	5,729	5,578	8,319
MARYLAND	5,071,604	170,052	3,494,905	141,828	3,353,077	1,373,129	15,343	188,227
MASSACHU-SETTS	6,092,352	348,181	5,499,644	275,693	5,223,951	377,715	14,279	200,714
MICHIGAN	9,594,350	242,128	8,024,496	215,033	7,809,463	1,368,804	58,939	142,111
MINNESOTA	4,657,758	76,044	4,360,889	65,814	4,295,075	128,056	56,934	111,879
MISSISSIPPI	2,716,115	20,149	1,702,058	15,988	1,686,070	986,895	9,638	17,524
MISSOURI	5,358,692	76,755	4,685,274	67,767	4,617,507	597,565	20,418	55,435
MONTANA	879,372	14,550	816,791	12,244	804,547	3,216	54,226	5,139
NEBRASKA	1,652,093	63,294	1,552,364	57,640	1,494,724	64,953	14,744	20,032
NEVADA	1,603,163	226,039	1,388,507	205,786	1,182,721	118,440	28,120	68,096
NEW HAMP-SHIRE	1,162,481	15,852	1,139,475	14,391	1,125,084	8,066	2,281	12,659
NEW JERSEY	7,987,933	920,085	6,414,926	792,965	5,621,961	1,157,171	20,622	395,214
NEW MEXICO	1,713,407	677,341	1,490,295	649,808	840,487	43,001	157,181	22,930
NEW YORK	18,184,774	2,537,597	13,991,765	1,916,575	12,075,190	3,198,235	72,963	921,811
NORTH CARO-LINA	7,322,870	134,384	5,518,807	114,871	5,403,936	1,624,259	93,963	85,841
NORTH DAKOTA	643,539	6,359	604,844	5,326	599,518	4,111	29,392	5,192
OHIO	11,172,782	168,711	9,766,839	149,373	9,617,466	1,264,493	22,356	110,094
OKLAHOMA	3,300,902	114,823	2,745,517	95,578	2,649,939	253,319	260,501	41,565
OREGON	3,203,735	177,233	3,005,721	162,308	2,843,413	57,752	44,116	96,146
PENNSYLVANIA	12,056,112	292,050	10,690,370	245,200	10,445,170	1,162,462	17,067	186,213
RHODE ISLAND	990,225	59,475	917,164	47,509	869,655	47,050	4,683	21,328
SOUTH CARO-LINA	3,698,746	40,771	2,543,890	33,747	2,510,143	1,115,869	8,754	30,233
SOUTH DAKOTA	732,405	7,266	666,157	5,782	660,375	4,542	57,221	4,485
TENNESSEE	5,319,654	52,302	4,385,463	44,667	4,340,796	874,592	11,843	47,756
TEXAS	19,128,261	5,503,372	16,203,786	5,309,635	10,894,151	2,336,165	90,035	498,275
UTAH	2,000,494	121,641	1,907,846	112,675	1,795,171	16,747	28,472	47,429
VERMONT	588,654	5,704	578,103	5,195	572,908	3,500	1,695	5,356
VIRGINIA	6,675,451	223,828	5,111,445	195,348	4,916,097	1,322,722	17,780	223,504
WASHINGTON	5,532,939	321,684	4,944,646	284,864	4,659,782	189,241	99,369	299,683
WEST VIRGINIA	1,825,754	9,892	1,756,915	8,790	1,748,125	57,600	2,544	8,695
WISCONSIN	5,159,795	122,622	4,756,004	109,880	4,646,124	284,368	45,277	74,146
WYOMING	481,400	27,536	463,029	25,578	437,451	4,082	10,558	3,731

Note: In the categories given above, American Indian includes Eskimo and Aleut

Source: Administrative Records and Methodology Research Branch—U.S. Bureau of the Census

5. Major Events in United States History

1700

1754 — French and Indian War
Boston Tea Party — 1773
1776 — Declaration of Independence
Slavery is illegal in Massachusetts — 1783
1789 — George Washington becomes President
Building of the White House starts — 1792

1800

— Federal government moves to Washington, D.C.
War of 1812 — 1812
1845 — Texas becomes a state
Gold discovered in California — 1848
1861 — Civil War begins
Lincoln frees the slaves — 1863
1865 — Civil War ends

1900

San Francisco earthquake — 1906
1917 — World War I begins
Word War II begins — 1941
1955 — Supreme Court orders school integration
President John F. Kennedy is killed — 1963
1968 — Martin Luther King, Jr. is killed
200th Anniversary of U.S. independence — 1976
1995 — Oklahoma City terrorist bombing

6. Weights and Measures, Temperatures (Celsius and Fahrenheit)

Weights and Measures

1 pound (lb.) = 453.6 grams (g.)
16 ounces (oz.) = 1 pound (lb.)
2,000 pounds (lb.) = 1 ton

1 inch (in. or ″) = 2.54 centimeters (cm)
1 foot (ft or ′) = 0.3048 meters (m)
12 inches (12″) = 1 foot (1′)
3 feet (3′) = 1 yard (yd.)
1 mile = 5,280 feet (5,280′)

Temperature chart: Celsius and Fahrenheight

degrees (°) Celsius (C) = ⅝ degrees Fahrenheight) − 32

degrees (°) Fahrenheight (C) = ⅝ degrees Celsius) + 32

C:	100°	30°	25°	20°	15°	10°	5°	0°	−5°
F:	212°	86°	77°	68°	59°	50°	41°	32°	23°

7. Native American Population— 1980 vs. 1990

Tribe	1990 Census		1980 Census	
	Number	**Percent**	**Number**	**Percent**
All American Indians	1,937,391	100.0	1,478,523	100.0
Cherokee	369,035	19.0	232,080	15.7
Navajo	225,298	11.6	158,633	10.7
Sioux 1	107,321	5.5	78,608	5.3
Chippewa	105,988	5.5	73,602	5.0
Choctaw	86,231	4.5	50,220	3.4
Pueblo 2	55,330	2.9	42,552	2.9
Apache	53,330	2.8	35,861	2.4
Iroquois 3	52,557	2.7	38,218	2.6
Lumbee 4	50,888	2.6	28,631	1.9
Creek	45,872	2.4	28,278	1.9
Blackfoot 2	37,992	2.0	21,964	1.5
Canadian and Latin American	27,179	1.4	7,804	0.5
Chickasaw	21,522	1.1	10,317	0.7
Tohono O'Odham	16,876	0.9	13,297	0.9
Potawatomi	16,719	0.9	9,715	0.7
Seminole 2	15,564	0.8	10,363	0.7
Pima	15,074	0.8	11,722	0.8
Tlingit	14,417	0.7	9,509	0.6
Alaskan Athabaskans	14,198	0.7	10,136	0.7
Cheyenne	11,809	0.6	9,918	0.7
Comanche	11,437	0.6	9,037	0.6
Paiute 2	11,369	0.6	9,523	0.6
Osage	10,430	0.5	6,884	0.5
Puget Sound Salish	10,384	0.5	6,591	0.4
Yaqui	9,838	0.5	5,197	0.4

Source: Bureau of Census, Washington, D.C.

8. United States Wealth and Poverty by State

Poverty = annual income of less than $15,141 for a family of four
Per Capita Income = average annual income per person

State	Percent of Persons in Poverty	Per Capita Personal Income ($)
United States	14.0	25,598
Alabama	16.8	20,842
Alaska	8.5	25,305
Arizona	15.8	22,364
Arkansas	17.5	19,585
California	17.2	26,570
Colorado	9.5	27,051
Connecticut	10.7	36,263
Delaware	9.1	29,022
D.C.	22.5	35,852
Florida	15.1	25,255
Georgia	13.6	24,061
Hawaii	10.4	26,034
Idaho	12.8	20,478
Illinois	12.3	28,202
Indiana	10.3	23,604
Iowa	10.8	23,102
Kansas	12.3	24,379
Kentucky	16.7	20,657
Louisiana	22.0	20,680
Maine	10.6	22,078
Maryland	10.4	28,969
Massachusetts	10.3	31,524
Michigan	12.5	25,560
Minnesota	10.2	26,797
Mississippi	21.3	18,272
Missouri	11.5	24,001
Montana	14.6	20,046
Nebraska	9.5	23,803
Nevada	10.1	26,791
New Hampshire	6.5	28,047
New Jersey	8.7	32,654
New Mexico	24.0	19,587
New York	16.7	30,752
North Carolina	11.1	23,345
North Dakota	11.1	20,271
Ohio	12.8	24,661
Oklahoma	16.8	20,556
Oregon	11.6	24,393
Pennsylvania	16.8	26,058
Rhode Island	10.6	25,760
South Carolina	15.6	20,775
South Dakota	13.6	21,447
Tennessee	15.3	23,018
Texas	17.7	23,656
Utah	8.0	20,432
Vermont	10.2	23,401
Virginia	11.1	26,483

State	Percent of Persons in Poverty	Per Capita Personal Income ($)
Washington	12.0	26,718
West Virginia	17.9	18,957
Wisconsin	8.8	24,475
Wyoming	11.1	22,648

Source: Bureau of the Census, Washington, D.C.

9. List of Presidents and years in office

George Washington	1789–1797
John Adams	1797–1801
Thomas Jefferson	1801–1809
James Madison	1809–1817
James Monroe	1817–1825
John Quincy Adams	1825–1829
Andrew Jackson	1829–1837
Martin Van Buren	1837–1841
William Henry Harrison	1841
John Tyler	1841–1845
James Polk	1845–1849
Zachary Taylor	1849–1850
Millard Fillmore	1850–1853
Franklin Pierce	1853–1857
James Buchanan	1857–1861
Abraham Lincoln	1861–1865
Andrew Johnson	1865–1869
Ulysses S. Grant	1869–1877
Rutherford B. Hayes	1877–1881
James A. Garfield	1881
Chester A. Arthur	1881–1885
Grover Cleveland	1885–1889
Benjamin Harrison	1889–1893
Grover Cleveland	1893–1897
William McKinley	1897–1901
Theodore Roosevelt	1901–1909
William H. Taft	1909–1913
Woodrow Wilson	1913–1921
Warren Harding	1921–1923
Calvin Coolidge	1923–1929
Herbert Hoover	1929–1933
Franklin D. Roosevelt	1933–1945
Harry S. Truman	1945–1953
Dwight D. Eisenhower	1953–1961
John F. Kennedy	1961–1963
Lyndon B. Johnson	1963–1969
Richard M. Nixon	1969–1974
Gerald R. Ford	1974–1977
Jimmy Carter	1977–1981
Ronald W. Reagan	1981–1989
George Bush	1989–1993
William J. Clinton	1993–2001

10. List of First Ladies of the United States of America

First Lady	Born	Died
Martha Dandridge Custis Washington	1731	1802
Abigail Smith Adams	1744	1818
Martha Wayles Skelton Jefferson	1748	1782
Dolley Payne Todd Madison	1768	1849
Elizabeth Kortright Monroe	1768	1830
Louisa Catherine Johnson Adams	1775	1852
Rachel Donelson Jackson	1767	1828
Hannah Hoes Van Buren	1783	1819
Anna Tuthill Symmes Harrison	1775	1864
Letitia Christian Tyler	1790	1842
Julia Gardiner Tyler	1820	1889
Sarah Childress Polk	1803	1891
Margaret Mackall Smith Taylor	1788	1852
Abigail Powers Fillmore	1798	1853
Jane Means Appleton Pierce	1806	1863
Harriet Lane	1830	1903
Mary Todd Lincoln	1818	1882
Eliza McCardle Johnson	1810	1876
Julia Dent Grant	1826	1902
Lucy Ware Webb Hayes	1831	1889
Lucretia Rudolph Garfield	1832	1918
Ellen Lewis Herndon Arthur	1837	1880
Frences Folsom Cleveland	1864	1947
Caroline Lavina Scott Harrison	1832	1892
Ida Saxton McKinley	1847	1907
Edith Kermit Carow Roosevelt	1861	1948
Helen Herron Taft	1861	1943
Ellen Louise Axson Wilson	1860	1914
Edith Bolling Galt Wilson	1872	1961
Florence Kling Harding	1860	1924
Grace Anna Goodhue Coolidge	1879	1957
Lou Henry Hoover	1874	1944
Anna Eleanor Roosevelt Roosevelt	1884	1962
Elizabeth Virginia Wallace Truman	1885	1982
Mamie Geneva Doud Eisenhower	1896	1979
Jacqueline Lee Bouvier Kennedy Onassis	1929	1994
Claudia Taylor Johnson	1912	
Patricia Ryan Nixon	1912	1993
Elizabeth Bloomer Ford	1918	
Rosalynn Smith Carter	1927	
Nancy Davis Reagan	1923	
Barbara Pierce Bush	1925	
Hillary Rodham Clinton	1947	

11. Television Watching Habits

Television Viewing Per U.S. Household

Year	Hours per day
1950	4:35
1955	4:51
1960	5:06
1965	5:29
1970	5:56
1975	6:18
1980	6:45
1985	7:10
1990	6:56

Most Popular TV Shows 1958, 1968, 1978, 1988, 1998

Top Five Shows 1958

Name of show	Type of show
1. The $64,000 Question	quiz show
2. I Love Lucy	situation comedy
3. The Ed Sullivan Show	variety show
4. Disneyland	children's show
5. The Jack Benny Show	comedy

Top Five Shows 1968

Name of show	Type of show
1. Laugh-in	comedy/variety
2. Gomer Pyle	situation comedy
3. Bonanza	western
4. Mayberry, R.F.D.	situation comedy
5. Family Affair	situation comedy

Top Five Shows 1978

Name of show	Type of show
1. Laverne and Shirley	situation comedy
2. Three's Company	situation comedy
3. Mork & Mindy	situation comedy
4. 60 Minutes	news
5. Charlie's Angels	crime drama

Top Five Shows 1988

Name of show	Type of show
1. The Cosby Show	situation comedy
2. Roseanne	situation comedy
3. A Different World	situation comedy
4. Cheers	situation comedy
5. 60 Minutes	news

Top Five Shows 1998

Name of show	Type of show
1. ER	medical drama
2. Frasier	situation comedy
3. Friends	situation comedy
4. Jesse	situation comedy
5. Veronica's Closet	situation comedy

12. Internet Information

Countries connected to the Internet

CODE	COUNTRY	Initial Connection
DZ	Algeria	04/94
AR	Argentina	10/90
AM	Armenia	06/94
AU	Australia	05/89
AT	Austria	06/90
BY	Belarus	02/95
BE	Belgium	05/90
BM	Bermuda	03/94
BR	Brazil	06/90
BG	Bulgaria	04/93
BF	Burkina Faso	10/94
CM	Cameroon	12/92
CA	Canada	07/88
CL	Chile	04/90
CN	China	04/94
CO	Colombia	04/94
CR	Costa Rica	01/93
HR	Croatia	11/91
CY	Cyprus	12/92
CZ	Czech Republic	11/91
DK	Denmark	11/88
DO	Dominican Republic	04/95
EC	Ecuador	07/92
EG	Egypt	11/93
EE	Estonia	07/92
FJ	Fiji	06/93
FI	Finland	11/88
FR	France	07/88
PF	French Polynesia	10/94
DE	Germany	09/89
GH	Ghana	05/93
GR	Greece	07/90
GU	Guam	10/93
HK	Hong Kong	09/91
HU	Hungary	11/91
IS	Iceland	11/88

CODE	COUNTRY	Initial Connection
IN	India	11/90
ID	Indonesia	07/93
IE	Ireland	07/90
IL	Israel	08/89
IT	Italy	08/89
JM	Jamaica	05/94
JP	Japan	08/89
KZ	Kazakhstan	11/93
KE	Kenya	11/93
KR	Korea, South	04/90
KW	Kuwait	12/92
LV	Latvia	11/92
LB	Lebanon	06/94
LI	Liechtenstein	06/93
LT	Lithuania	04/94
LU	Luxembourg	04/92
MO	Macau	04/94
MY	Malaysia	11/92
MX	Mexico	02/89
MA	Morocco	10/94
MZ	Mozambique	03/95
NL	Netherlands	01/89
NC	New Caledonia	10/94
NZ	New Zealand	04/89
NI	Nicaragua	02/94
NE	Niger	10/94
NO	Norway	11/88
PA	Panama	06/94
PE	Peru	11/93
PH	Philippines	04/94
PL	Poland	11/91
PT	Portugal	10/91
PR	Puerto Rico	10/89
RO	Romania	04/93
RU	Russian Federation	06/93
SN	Senegal	10/94
SG	Singapore	05/91
SK	Slovakia	03/92
SI	Slovenia	02/92
ZA	South Africa	12/91
ES	Spain	07/90
SZ	Swaziland	05/94
SE	Sweden	11/88
CH	Switzerland	03/90
TW	Taiwan	12/91
TH	Thailand	07/92
TN	Tunisia	05/91

Source: http://NIC.MERIT.EDU

13. Fast Food Facts

American Fast Food Sales Figures

Year	Fast Food Sales
1980	$28,699,000,000
1985	$47,477,000,000
1990	$69,458,000,000
1995	$93,864,000,000

Source: Statistical Abstract of the U.S.

Fast Food Competitors (1998 figures)

Name	Restaurants Worldwide	Restaurants U.S. only
McDonald's	23,000	12,400
Burger King	9,644	7,539

Source: corporate web sites

14. Irregular Past Tenses and Past Participles

Simple Form	Past	Past Participle
be	was, were	been
become	became	become
begin	began	begun
bite	bit	bitten
blow	blew	blown
break	broke	broken
bring	brought	brought
buy	bought	bought
cost	cost	cost
do	did	done
drink	drank	drunk
drive	drove	driven
feel	felt	felt
fit	fit	fit
fly	flew	flown
get	got	gotten
give	gave	given
go	went	gone
have	had	had
hide	hid	hidden
hit	hit	hit
know	knew	known
lay	laid	laid
let	let	let
lie (down)	lay	lain
lie (untruth)	lied	lied
pay	paid	paid
read	read	read
ride	rode	ridden
shut	shut	shut
steal	stole	stolen
take	took	taken
teach	taught	taught
wake	woke	woken
wear	wore	worn

15. Common Prefixes and Suffixes

Common Prefixes

Prefix	Meaning	Example
after-	after	aftertaste
ambi-	both	ambidextrous
anti-	against	antiwar
aqua-	water	aquarium
audi-	sound	auditorium
auto-	self	autobiography
bi-	two	bilingual
co-	with	cooperate
dis-	negative of	disappear
ex-	in the past	ex-wife
hemi-	half	hemisphere
im-	not	immature
inter-	between, among	international
intra-	within	intrastate
micro-	small	microscope
multi-	many	multiracial
non-	not	nonsense
post-	after	postwar
re-	again	remember
un-	not	unusual
zoo-	animal	zoology

Common Suffixes

Suffix	Meaning	Example
-an	belonging to	American
-arium	place, building	aquarium
-chrome	color	monochrome
-en	consisting of	wooden
-er	person who does an action	writer
-ese	relating to	Japanese
-est	most	biggest
-gram	written	telegram
-graph	written	autograph
-ion	process	communication
-meter	measuring device	speedometer
-ness	quality	rudeness
-phone	sound	telephone
-sphere	globelike	hemisphere
-ster	one who is	youngster
-ward	direction	backward
-wide	extent	worldwide

TEXT CREDITS

(**Page 2**) Columbus cartoon from *Cartoon History of the U.S.* Copyright [c.] 1991 by Larry Gonick. Reprinted by permission of the author.

(**Page 3**) "Paradise." Public Domain.

(**Page 4**) "The New World." Public Domain.

(**Page 7**) "The Spirit of the Land." Public Domain.

(**Page 8**) "Civilization." Public Domain.

(**Page 13**) "Yokohama, California." Copyright [c.] 1949 by Toshio Mori, *Yokohama, California*. The Caxton Printers, Ltd., Caldwell, Idaho.

(**Page 16**) "Outside Fargo, North Dakota." From *Shall We Gather at the River*, Copyright [c.] 1968, Wesleyan University Press.

(**Page 21**) "Your Dream House." From *USA Today*, August, 1997. Copyright [c.] 1997, USA Today. Reprinted by permission.

(**Page 29**) "E-Mail Messages." From *The Dilbert Principle* by Scott Adams. Copyright [c.] 1996 by United Features Syndicate, Inc. Reprinted by permission of HarperCollins Publishers, Inc.

(**Page 34**) "Sabotage in the Workplace." Excerpted from *Sabotage in the American Workplace*, edited by Martin Sprouse. Copyright [c.] 1992 Pressure Drop Press.

(**Page 48**) "Cycle." From *The Atlantic Monthly*, May 1996. Copyright [c.] 1996. Reprinted by permission of the author.

(**Page 51**) "Smooth or Chunky." Copyright, USA Today. Reprinted with permission.

(**Page 66**) "Rosa Parks." From the website of the Academy of Achievement: *www.achievement.org*. Copyright [c.] 1998 Reprinted by permission of the Academy of Achievement.

(**Page 71**) "Born to Run Free" Reprinted with permission form the 75th Anniversary Issue of *Reader's Digest*. Copyright [c.] 1997 by The Reader's Digest Assn., Inc.

(**Page 75**) "Fox Trot." Copyright by Universal Press Syndicate. Reprint by permission of Universal Press Syndicate. All rights reserved.

(**Page 76**) "Mother's Stories." Contributed by Phyllis Laxton (May, 1986), William H. Speidel (October, 1990) and Jane C. Sutton (November 1984). *Reader's Digest*, May 1986. Copyright [c.] 1986 by The Reader's Digest Association, Inc.

(**Page 79**) "Mother's Day Special." From *State of the Union*, Copyright [c.] 1997. Reprinted by permission of Wisconsin Public Television.

(**Page 87**) "America's Main Street." Copyright [c.] 1990 by Michael Wallis. From *Route 66: The Mother Road* by Michael Wallis. Reprinted by permission of St. Martin's Press, Incorporated.

(**Page 91**) "Mississippi Monte Carlo." From *The Atlantic Monthly*, January 1996. Copyright [c.] 1996. Reprinted by permission of the author.

(**Page 96**) "The Best Places to Raise a Family." Reprinted with permission from the April 1997 *Reader's Digest*. Copyright [c.] 1997 by the Reader's Digest Assn., Inc.

(**Page 101**) "The Suburban Century." Excerpted for *The Atlantic Monthly*, July 1992. Copyright [c.] 1992. Reprinted with permission of the author.

(**Page 109**) "English Only Laws." Reprinted with permission of the American Civil Liberties Union.

(**Page 114**) "English Language Education for Immigrant Children." Reprinted by permission of **One** Nation/One California.

(**Page 119**) "Lingo or Language?" Copyright [c.] 1997 The San Antonio News. Reprinted by permission of the San Antonio Express News.

(**Page 130**) "The Flag Code." Public Domain.

(**Page 144**) "The Lincoln Bedroom." From Millie's Book. Copyright [c.] 1990 by Barbara Bush Foundation for Family. Reprinted by permission of William Morrow & Company, Inc.

(**Page 151**) "Dolly Parton." From: *www.vamprod.force9.uk/Dolly/*. Copyright [c.] 1997. Reprinted by permission of the author.

(**Page 154**) "Robert." Copyright [c.] 1969 Velvet Apple Music. All rights reserved. Used by permission.

(**Page 154**) "Heartbreak Hotel." By Mae Boren Axton, Tommy Durden and Elvis Presley. Copyright [c.] Sony/ATV Songs LLC (Renewed). All rights administered by Sony/ATV Music Publishing, 8 Music Square West, Nashville, TN 37203. All rights reserved.

(**Page 160**) "Calvin and Hobbes" Copyright by Universal Press Syndicate. Reprint by permission of Universal Press Syndicate. All rights reserved.

(**Page 162**) "The Far Side" Copyright by Universal Press Syndicate. Reprinted by permission of Universal Press Syndicate. All rights reserved.

(**Page 163**) "Dilbert." Copyright by United Feature Syndicate, Inc. Reprinted by permission of United Feature Syndicate, Inc.

(**Page 168**) "Other Seniors Eager for Space." Copyright [c.] 1998 by the Associated Press.

(**Page 172**) "Mission to the Moon" From *Time for Kids*, January 16, 1998. Copyright [c.] 1998 Time Inc. Reprinted by permission.

(**Page 178**) "The Rules of Netiquette." From *Netiquette* by Virginia Shea. Copyright [c.] 1994 Virginia Shea. Reprinted with permission of Albion Books (www.albion.com)

(**Page 182**) "Net Addiction" Copyright [c.] 1996 by The New York Times. Reprinted by permission.

(**Page 189**) "Unplugged." Copyright [c.] 1994 by Highlights for Children, Inc. Columbus, Ohio.

(**Page 193**) "I Love Lucy." Lyric by Harold Adamson. Music by Eliot Daniel. Copyright [c.] 1953 (Renewed), DESILU MUSIC CORP. All rights reserved.

(**Page 197**) "To Kill a Mockingbird." (novel) [c.] 1960 by Harper Lee. "To Kill A Mockingbird" (screenplay) [c.] 1964 by Boardwalk Productions and Brentwood Productions, Inc. "To Kill A Mockingbird" (screenplay) [c.] 1992 by Horton Foote.

(**Page 202**) "The Movie That Changed My Life." From *The Movie That Changed My Life*. Copyright [c.] 1991, Terry McMillan. Reprinted by permission of the author.

PHOTO CREDITS

(**Page 1**) UPI/Corbis-Bettmann

(**Page 2**) Larry Gonick

(**Page 6**) Library of Congress/Corbis

(**Page 12**) The Brett Weston Archive/Corbis

(**Page 15**) Richard Hamilton Smith/Corbis

(**Page 19**) UPI/Corbis-Bettmann

(**Page 28**) Heinle & Heinle Publishers

(**Page 33**) Roger Ressmeyer/Corbis

(**Page 41**) Heinle & Heinle Publishers

(**Page 42**) Brian McDermott

(**Page 47**) Owen Franken/Corbis

(**Page 51**) USA Today, Gannett Co. Inc.

(**Page 55**) Heinle & Heinle Publishers

(**Page 63**) Seth Joel/Corbis

(**Page 66**) UPI/Corbis-Bettmann

(**Page 70**) Peter Johnson/Corbis

(**Page 75**) Universal Press Syndicate, Inc.

(**Page 78**) Seth Joel/Corbis

(**Page 85**) Heinle & Heinle Publishers

(**Page 86**) Joseph Sohm; ChromoSohm Inc./Corbis

(**Page 100**) Matt Groening Productions, Inc.

(**Page 107**) Heinle & Heinle Publishers

(**Page 127**) Ted Spiegel/Corbis

(**Page 134**) Leif Skoogfors/Corbis

(**Page 136**) Schenectady Museum – Hall of Electrical History/Corbis

(**Page 139**) Richard T. Nowitz/Corbis

(**Page 141**) James P. Blair/Corbis

(**Page 143**) Bush Presidential Materials Project/Corbis

(**Page 149**) Corbis-Bettmann

(**Page 151**) Michael Gerber/Corbis

(**Page 156**) EPI/Corbis-Bettmann

(**Page 160**) Universal Press Syndicate, Inc.

(**Page 162**) Universal Press Syndicate, Inc.

(**Page 163**) United Feature Syndicate, Inc.

(**Page 165**) Michael Burggren

(**Page 169**) New America Publications, Inc.

(**Page 171**) UPI/Corbis-Bettmann

(**Page 187**) UPI/Corbis-Bettmann

(**Page 192**) UPI/Corbis-Bettmann

(**Page 196**) UPI/Corbis-Bettmann

(**Page 201**) UPI/Corbis-Bettmann